KEY

S0-BCQ-625

🚇 Underground

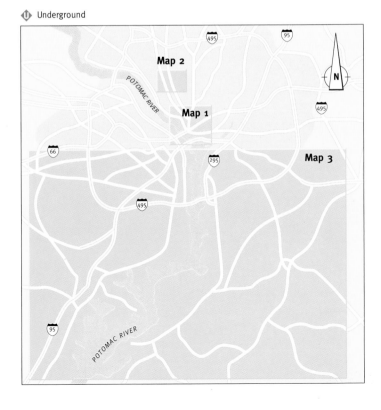

First North American Edition

ISBN 0-8212-2233-3

Library of Congress Catalog Card Number 95-76700

Bulfinch Press is an imprint and trademark of Little, Brown and Company (Inc.) Published simultaneously in Canada by Little, Brown & Company (Canada) Limited

PRINTED IN SPAIN

ART IN focus

Washington

WASHINGTON

Nicholas Reese

A Bulfinch Press Book
Little, Brown and Company
Boston • New York • Toronto • London

CONTENTS

CONTENTS

In his address at a ceremony for the inauguration of the Smithsonian's Hirshhorn Museum in May 1966, President Lyndon Johnson proclaimed: 'Washington is a city of powerful institutions; the seat of government for the strongest nation on earth, the place where democratic ideals are translated into reality. It must also be a place of beauty and learning. Its buildings and thoroughfares, its schools, concert halls and museums should reflect a people whose commitment is to the best that is within them to dream. In the National Gallery collection, in the Freer and the Corcoran Galleries, in the museums of the Smithsonian, and now in the Hirshhorn Museum and Sculpture Garden, we have the elements of a great capital of beauty and learning no less impressive than its power.'

Although his speech is embellished with conventional presidential rhetoric, Johnson summed up the particular character of Washington as the centre of government of a vast and disparate nation which is also the most economically and politically powerful country in the world. Washington is a city of symbols and a focus for national identity. It is also the exemplary governmental city where grandiose and often faceless buildings housing great state departments flank many of the main thoroughfares. Over the river, the Pentagon with its forbidding vastness is perhaps the ultimate architectural symbol of power beyond the comprehension of the individual, and the Federal Reserve Bank, whose policies mould world financial markets, is also based in the city. The visitor is constantly aware that this is a city which lives and breathes power, but it is to the great credit of its architects that this power is presented with a beautiful facade. The city has been thoughtfully planned so that side by side with the monumental government offices, are museums of art, science and history; an ensemble which has no parallel elsewhere.

1. GEORGIA O'KEEFFE, *GOATS HORN WITH RED*, 1945 (HIRSCHHORN MUSEUM OF ART)

2. Leonardo Da Vinci, *Ginevra Di Benci*, c. 1480 (National Gallery of Art)

3. Bartolomé Esteban Murillo, *A Young Girl With Her Duenna*, c. 1655/60 (National Gallery of Art)

That the city of big government should at the same time be the centre of a great concentration of cultural resources is perhaps no surprise, but the story behind the evolution of the collections is an interesting and astonishing one. It took a surprisingly long time for the notion of the city as a cultural centre to take form, and yet once it was established collections of outstanding quality were assembled with amazing rapidity. This is in no small part due to the energy, munificence and above all wealth, of a small number of remarkable individual patrons. 'Enlightened philanthropy has always been an essential part of American life since the founding of the Republic' wrote Arthur M. Sackler, who himself made a major contribution to the wealth of the collections in the city. Behind all the public museums in Washington lurk generous and enlightened benefactors, whose magnanimity could earn them a modicum of immortality through the continuation of art appreciation and learning. For the art lover it is these collections which are the city's main draw and one in particular, the National Gallery of Art, is one of the greatest collections of Western art in the world. There is also the attraction of the civic buildings and monuments which embellish Washington and the grand conception of its overall plan. Finally, there is much in Washington to appreciate from its Colonial and Federal past; in particular the excursions from the city centre include some of the finest and certainly most famous Colonial sites in the nation.

A little should be said about the evolution of the capital, for Washington is a city built from scratch and should be appreciated as a masterpiece of town planning. Prior to the Revolutionary War the site upon which Washington is now located was little more than a swamp beside the river Potomac. The nearby towns of Alexandria and Georgetown were trading centres serving the largely agrarian populations of Virginia and Maryland.

The fledgling nation was born out of great ideals and as the result of a hard fought war for independence from its colonial overlords. Not least of the problems facing the founding fathers was how to unite the thirteen former colonies, now quasi-independent states, which had fought together to break free of the yoke of British rule to form a peaceful and prosperous nation. The choice of a capital was an important one. In the years following its inception, the Continental Congress, which constituted the government of the country, had met in no less than eight different cities including both New York and Philadelphia, and it was decided that it needed a permanent home, not least to placate the rivalry between the well established cities. The site of Washington was eventually decided upon. This was to a great extent owing to the personality of George Washington himself, whose estates at Mount Vernon were located a short distance away along the Potomac. Its position between the cities of the north and the agricultural states to the south was a crucial factor, and the fact that it lay on the Potomac river allowing access to shipping was another advantage. Further, the land was ceded by the state of Maryland on the basis that the Federal government only had to pay for the sites it actually chose for its buildings rather than the complete territory.

In 1791 Washington, after whom the Congress decided to name the city, appointed Pierre Charles L'Enfant as the chief town planner. At the same time the diamond-shaped expanse of land given over to the building of the capital was named the Territory (later District) of Columbia. The city developed, and by 1800 was far enough advanced to become the capital of the United States. Although it was still not much more than an outline of the future city, it was politically expedient that the President and other officials of state establish themselves there. In August 1814, during the war with the British, Washington was invaded and numerous public buildings, including the White House and Capitol, were burned down. This major setback was overcome, albeit slowly, and Washington developed in line with the nation's expansion.

Perhaps the best indication of Washington's character in the nineteenth century was given by Charles Dickens, who wrote when he visited the city in the 1840s: 'It is sometimes called the city of magnificent distances, but it might with greater propriety be termed the city of magnificent intentions......Spacious avenues that begin in nothing and lead nowhere; streets a mile long that only want houses, roads and inhabitants; public meetings that need but a public to be complete; and ornaments of great thoroughfares that only lack great thoroughfares to ornament.'

4. TITIAN, *RANUCCIO FARNESE*, 1542 (NATIONAL GALLERY OF ART)

5. GILBERT STUART, *GEORGE WASHINGTON*, 1796 (NATIONAL PORTRAIT GALLERY)

6. Jan Vermeer, *The Girl With The Red Hat*, 1665–67 (National Gallery of Art)

Although doubtless exaggerated for literary effect, this description conveys something of the character of a city trying to develop and forge an identity when other cities in the union, notably New York and Philadelphia, were booming through a massive wave of immigration and industrial development. Washington remained a backwater harbouring dreams and with great potential. One individual with a dream and foresight was the Hon. Joel R. Poinsett, the Secretary of War after whom the Poinsettia flower was named. He wrote in 1841 that the arts should be encouraged, emphasizing that this encouragement 'must originate at the seat of government'. The idea was that the city should be not only the political focal point of the nation but a cultural one as well. The basis for this cultural development had in fact been made some years before when James Smithson, an Englishman who never visited America, had somewhat mysteriously bequeathed half a million dollars to the United States. This laid the foundation for the Smithsonian Institution, a unique and remarkable organization and the hub of scientific, historical and artistic activity

7. Edward Hopper, *Cape Cod, Evening*, 1939 (National Gallery of Art)

One of the most successful of all planned cities, Washington is an outstanding example of eighteenth-century town planning and a work of art in its own right. The concept of the city largely stemmed from the mind of Pierre Charles L'Enfant (1754–1825). An irascible and colourful character, L'Enfant arrived in America at the age of twenty-two after training in Paris. He served in the revolutionary army under Washington and subsequently established himself as an architect and designer and ingratiated himself with his former commander, impressing him with his ideas for the planning of the new capital.

An important initial decision was to locate the future Congress House on the top of Jenkins Hill, a small promontory which commanded a view over the Potomac river. Now known as Capitol Hill or more simply as 'The Hill' this is the centre from which the plan of the city radiates. Although the city was initially to be built towards the east, it was in fact laid out over swamp land to the west with an avenue 400 feet wide intended to be lined by foreign ministries and cultural institutions.

This avenue, now called the Mall, was to culminate with an equestrian statue of George Washington. Running north and south would be a further axis at the northern apex of which would be the proposed President's house, linked with the Capitol by a mile-long commercial corridor, present-day Pennsylvania Avenue.

The remainder of the city was laid out in a grid pattern of streets intersected by wide diagonal avenues emanating from specific round points, creating a general effect of a pattern of diagonals overlain on a chess board. The emphasis was on mighty vistas culminating in monumental buildings.

A series of conflicts resulted in L'Enfant's dismissal by Washington in February 1792, and the Frenchman died in poverty thirty-three years later. However, his scheme still remains the basis for the city as we see it today, and it is worth taking a visit to the Western Plaza on Pennsylvania Avenue below 13th and 14th streets, where the paving has a marble reproduction of the L'Enfant's original plan.

8. VIEW TOWARDS
THE CAPITOL

in Washington but with a significance which extends far beyond the capital (and indeed the nation).

Politically, the position of Washington changed in the second half of the nineteenth century along with that of the United States. The government in Washington had fought to preserve the Union in a bloody civil war which raged for five years and which claimed more American lives than any other before or since. With the Union preserved, the Federal government and its capital Washington D.C. increased in importance. Washington also by degrees became the capital of one of the richest, most powerful and certainly fastest growing, nations in the world.

The founding in 1869 of the Corcoran Art Gallery (page 21) began the development of the city into a centre for the fine arts, and by the end of the century some enlightened individuals were beginning to talk about a National Gallery in Washington D.C. In 1891 Franklin Webster Smith brought out a publication entitled *A design and prospectus for National Galleries for History and Art in Washington*. Despite being very much an amateur, Smith's proposals met with some enthusiasm among members of the Congress. At the same time the Smithsonian, which was primarily concerned with matters scientific, was beginning to devote some of its energy towards the fine arts. In 1906 it was decided in the courts that the Smithsonian should be the beneficiary of the Harriet Lane Johnston art collection. More significant was the bequest to the Smithsonian by Charles Lang Freer, the Detroit railroad car magnate of his own outstanding collection of Oriental and American art, together with a building erected on the Mall and an endowment for the expansion of the collection through acquisition and a foundation for research and scholarship.

The Freer (page 31) remains one of the great Oriental art galleries of the United States and the endowment obviously encouraged those who wished to establish a similar gallery devoted to Western art. Foremost among these was Andrew Mellon. The National Gallery's west building

9. J. A. M. WHISTLER, *THE GOLDEN SCREEN*, 1864 (FREER GALLERY OF ART)

was paid for and built by Mellon, who endowed it with his magnificent collection (page 55). Yet behind its wonderful inventory of Old Masters lurks the figure of Lord Duveen, whose dealership supplied so many of the paintings, not only those from Andrew Mellon but also Samuel Kress and others. It was Duveen who had encouraged Mellon to realize his dream and who persuaded him to use John Russell Pope as architect. Mellon also made the important decision that the gallery be sheltered under the banner of the Smithsonian Institution, which enabled it to benefit from government protection independent from political interference. He was also insistent that the museum he founded should not bear his name, even though it was very much his conception and was filled with his paintings and sculptures. The reason for this was very sound, for he was anxious that the gallery should attract bequests from other collectors and that his paintings should not overshadow any others. The National Gallery of Art was considered the most appropriate and prestigious name. Attract other collectors it did, as well as generous financial endowments to enable further purchases. Remarkable bequests followed that of the founder: Old Master paintings belonging to Samuel Kress and his brother Rush, the Wideners of Philadelphia and Chester Dale, whom we have to thank for a large number of the Impressionist and Post-Impressionist paintings. The children of the founder, Paul Mellon and Alisa Mellon Bruce also become two of its greatest benefactors, and there are many more whose generosity and work have created a museum which has few peers.

Washington attracted fortunes, and with fortunes came great art. In a society whose classless ideal had meant greater opportunity for all, the accumulation of art was one way of establishing individual cultural superiority. Collecting art enabled the newly wealthy Americans to rival the old established European families in terms of their ownership of universally respected symbols of value and taste. Wealthy men and women were attracted to Washington through their connection with the government, and their collections came with them, and in line with the enlightened philanthropic tradition, they have passed into the public domain. This has been facilitated in part by the tax structure in the United States which encourages the benefaction of museums. Without this enviable fiscal regime, many of the treasures on display in Washington would remain in private hands. Apart from the National Gallery of Art, other museums began attracting generous bequests, in particular the gift from Montana copper king, William Clark, of his Old Master collection to the Corcoran Gallery.

10. Amedeo Modigliani, *Gypsy Woman With Baby*, 1919 (National Gallery of Art)

At a meeting in 1919, steel king Henry Clay Frick introduced the young Andrew Mellon to the art dealer Lord Duveen, 'This unassuming young man is Andrew Mellon, someday he will be the greatest collector of us all' he prophetically exclaimed. Mellon was born the sixth of eight children in March 1855, to a wealthy banking family in Pittsburgh. His exceptional fiscal acumen brought the family bank controlling interests in what was to become the Aluminium Corporation of America and Gulf Oil Corporation amongst other concerns, and by the beginning of the century he had acquired a vast fortune. In 1921 he was invited by President Harding to become chief secretary to the treasury, and for the next eight years the shy, quietly spoken Andrew Mellon made himself into the dominant figure in government, being described as 'One of the greatest constructive economists of the century'.

In 1932 Mellon resigned to become ambassador to Great Britain, which allowed him to devote more time to his collecting and realize his now paramount ambition, which was the founding of the National Gallery of Art in Washington. He had nurtured this vision since the mid

11. THOMAS GAINSBOROUGH, *MRS. RICHARD BRINSLEY SHERIDAN*, 1785–87 (NATIONAL GALLERY OF ART)

1920s and had been collecting art from a young age under the guidance of Frick and Duveen among others. It was Duveen who showed him the possibilities which a government backed national collection could realize and he resolved to model his museum on the National Gallery in London. Duveen also supplied him with a good proportion of his collection, in particular thirty-six pictures which had been purchased by Duveen from the Dreyfus collection. Mellon's other greatest acquisition coup was his purchase of twenty-one masterpieces from the Soviet Union from 1927 to 1931, many of which had hung in the Hermitage Gallery in St Petersburg. In 1936 Mellon was brought to trial on charges relating to tax irregularities and although he was acquitted this was a rather sad episode in a glorious career. He died the following year, four years before the opening of the Gallery. His gift to the National Gallery of Art and his collection was, however, probably the greatest ever received by the nation from a single individual.

12. OSWALD BIRLEY, *ANDREW MELLON*, 1923 (NATIONAL PORTRAIT GALLERY)

13. PIERRE-AUGUSTE RENOIR, *THE LUNCHEON OF THE BOATING PARTY*, 1881 (THE PHILLIPS COLLECTION)

Since the end of World War One a number of highly personal private collections of very high quality have been opened to the public. Outstanding by any criteria is the Phillips Collection (page 106), a gallery which as much as any other shows the collector's great knowledge and passionate love of art. The same could be said of the Byzantine and pre-Columbian work on exhibition at Dumbarton Oaks in Georgetown (page 27) , the product of a lifetime's collecting by Mr. and Mrs. Robert Woods Bliss. Unique and of exceptional quality is the collection of Russian and French decorative art at Hillwood in the north Washington suburbs, accumulated by cereal heiress Margaret Merriweather Post (page 37).

New collections are still being opened to the public and existing ones supplemented. The visitor should be aware that in most of the great public museums, especially those under the banner of the Smithsonian, only a fraction of the holdings can be on display at any given time, so that exhibits have to be shown in rotation. Each decade sees Washington's cultural wealth in the visual arts increase by degrees. Since the establishment of the National Gallery of Art, it has been joined by the Hirshhorn Museum and Sculpture Garden (page 39) and the museums on the Quadrangle – the Sackler and the National Museum of African Art (pages 116 and 92). The National Museum of American Art (page 94) and National Portrait Gallery (page 101) were rehoused by the Smithsonian and there will soon be a museum for native Americans in the capital. These museums are seen as a public resource to be enjoyed by all Americans, and those administered by the Smithsonian are exceptional in the United States in having no entrance charge. Other new collections that have opened their doors to the public in recent years include the National Museum of Women in the Arts, which opened in 1987 (page 97) and the Kreeger Museum, inaugurated in 1994 (page 49).

It could be argued that today people visit Washington as much for the works of art as to see the White House or Arlington Cemetery. Washington has become, in the years since World War Two, possibly the greatest museum centre in the United States, and this coupled with its grand town plan embellished with historical monuments, has made it a centre for art and architectural appreciation to rival European and Asian cities which have thousands of years of history to draw upon.

14. Mughal Miniature of *Humayun Seated In A Landscape*, c. 1650 (Sackler Gallery of Art)

15. David Smith Display (National Gallery of Art)

The Smithsonian Institution is named after James Smithson, born in 1765, the illegitimate son of the Duke of Northumberland and Elizabeth Kate Macie, a woman of substantial means. During his lifetime, Smithson was a not insignificant scientist and thinker. He was one of the youngest ever fellows of the Royal Society and his work as a mineralogist resulted in an ore, Smithsonite, being named after him. When he died unmarried and without issue, his will was found to contain an extraordinary stipulation: his estate was to go to his nephew, but if his nephew were to die without heirs the bequest was to go to the United States of America. Six years later the nephew died without progeny and subsequently the money became the property of the nation to be used to 'found at Washington under the name of the Smithsonian Institution an Establishment for the increase and diffusion of knowledge among men'. In 1838 the funds in the form of 105 bags of gold sovereigns, worth at the time in excess of $500,000, were deposited in the Philadelphia Mint, and in 1846 a bill was passed through Congress creating an independent corporate entity – the 'Establishment' – which in effect constituted the Smithsonian Institution.

The plans for the establishment included the construction of a building with 'suitable rooms or halls for the reception and arrangement, upon a liberal scale, of objects of natural history, including a geological and mineralogical cabinet; also a chemical laboratory, a library, a gallery of art and the necessary lecture rooms.' The red sandstone building, designed by James Renwick, had turrets and battlements like a medieval fortress, earning the building the nickname of The Castle.

The Smithsonian institution now constitutes the largest complex of museums, art galleries and research facilities in the world. The range, quantity and quality of the material it owns is astounding. Covering virtually every area of human interest the museums now house over one hundred and thirty-seven million objects. New specimens and art objects are constantly being added to the collections.

16. THE CASTLE (SMITHSONIAN INSTITUTION)

ART

IN

FOCUS

Museums

Paintings

Applied Arts

Architecture

ANDERSON HOUSE

Built 1902–08

Address
2118, Massachusetts
Avenue, NW Washington
D.C.
℡ (202) 785 2040

Map reference
①

How to get there
Metro: Dupont Circle

Opening times
Daily 1–4. Closed Sun, Mon
and public holidays

Entrance fee
Free entrance

Tours
Guided tours available daily
by appointment

Among the imposing mansions largely housing embassies which line Massachusetts Avenue is the Anderson House, home of the Society of the Cincinnati. The Society was founded in 1783 as a patriotic institution by former army officers of the Revolutionary War. George Washington was the first President General of the organization named after Lucius Quintus Cincinnatus, a Roman hero who, like Washington himself, reluctantly came out of quiet retirement as a farmer to serve his country as a soldier.

The house is much younger than the Society, having been built between 1902 and 1908 for Larz Anderson, a career diplomat who was descended from an original member of the Society. It contains a fine collection of works of art reflecting opulent living in the early part of this century, a number of artefacts from the Revolutionary period, and some fine Chinese porcelain and jade. There is also an interesting collection of military portraits by such American artists as Gilbert Stuart, John Trumbull and George Catlin. Flemish tapestries adorn the walls in the dining room while the English parlour has some good English furniture.

Attached to the B'nai B'rith Jewish social service institution is a small though high quality museum dedicated to Jewish art and culture. The museum consists of a permanent collection of antique and contemporary ritual objects such as Torah implements, spice boxes, Esther scrolls, Hanukkah menorahs and Kiddish cups as well as antiquities and Jewish folk art. Most of the artefacts in the museum were donated by Joseph and Olyn Horwitz. A space in the gallery to the left of the entrance hall houses temporary exhibitions, largely of the work of contemporary Jewish artists. To the rear of the gallery is the Smallman sculpture garden.

Among the most significant treasures in the collection is the correspondence that took place in 1790 between George Washington and Moses Seixas, sexton of the Tauro Synagogue in Newport Rhode Island. In this, one of the most important documents in Jewish American history, Seixas spelled out a principle endorsed by Washington that ours is 'a government which happily gives to bigotry no sanction, to persecution no assistance', a maxim which forms the basis of religious and ethnic tolerance in the United States.

Another Jewish museum which is worth visiting is the Lillian and Albert Small Gallery of Jewish Art, which is situated in the Adams Israel Synagogue. The synagogue, a charming place of worship, was the first to be built in Washington in the 1870s. Located at 701 3rd street NW Washington DC, it mounts temporary exhibitions concentrating on the life and history of Washington's Jewish community and there is a small permanent display relating to the building itself.

Address
1640, Rhode Island Avenue NW, Washington D.C.
✆ (202) 857 6583

Map reference

How to get there
Metro: Farragut North or Dupont Circle

Opening times
Sun to Fri 10–5. Closed Sat and Federal and Jewish holidays

Entrance fee
Suggested donation: adults $2.00, children $1

Tours
Guided tours available by arrangement

THE CAPITOL

Built 1793–1863

Address
East end of Mall on Capitol
Hill Washington D.C.
✆ (202) 225 6827

Map reference

How to get there
Metro: Capitol South or
Union Station

Opening times
June to Labor Day: daily
9–8. Rest of the year: daily
9–4.30. Closed on major
holidays

Entrance fee
Free entrance

Tours
Guided tours available daily
every 25 minutes between
9 and 3.45

The magnificent dome of the Capitol dominates the city centre and is the fulcrum of the town planning concept initiated by L'Enfant. William Thornton was its first architect: he based his design on English Palladian principles, adding a shallow saucer dome inspired by the Pantheon. The cornerstone was laid by Washington in 1793 and by November 1800 President John Adams was able to address the Congress in the building for the first time. Only a fraction of the design had been built by this date, and Thornton's resignation led to his being replaced by Latrobe as chief architect. Latrobe modified the design and added some of the delightfully original decorative details, such as the tobacco and corn cob capitals in the interior. In 1814 the building was burned by the British and only heavy rainfall prevented its total destruction. Building continued until completion in 1863.

Of all the interior rooms the Rotunda is the most impressive. Other highlights include four paintings by John Trumbull illustrating scenes from the Revolutionary War which he personally witnessed, the Statuary Hall, the Old Senate Chamber and the Old Supreme Court Chamber.

The oldest art gallery in the capital, this is also a notable school of art. It was founded in 1859 by William Wilson Corcoran, a self made philanthropist who had been born in Georgetown. He intended to set up the Gallery as a 'repository in the capital for portraits of American heroes and outstanding examples of contemporary American Art.' Moreover, he wanted to found a school of art which would allow future American painters to utilize the Gallery's permanent collection to perfect their own styles. Because of this, American artists believed it was a great honour to have their works included in the collection. Corcoran died in 1888, having gone some way towards fulfilling his aim of promoting and encouraging the 'American Genius.' Despite later acquisitions, the gallery still sees itself as being primarily an American collection.

The original building in which the collection was housed is now the Renwick Gallery (see page 115), part of the National Museum of American Art, but it is now accommodated in the same building as the school, built in 1893. In 1925 the Gallery received an outstanding bequest from the estate of Senator William Clark, the copper king of Montana, consisting of over two hundred Old Master paintings and drawings as well as the Louis XVI Salon, and some fine examples of the decorative arts. Clark's family also donated a sum of $700,000 to build an extension to the original building to house the bequest. This building was inaugurated in 1928, by which time another bequest of important European paintings from the collection of Edward and Mary Walker had entered the collection, including works by Renoir, Monet and Pissarro. Today it is one of the most pleasant of Washington galleries with fine exhibition space both for the permanent collection and temporary exhibitions.

Address
17th St and New York Avenue NW. Washington D.C.
✆ (202) 638 3211

Map reference

How to get there
Metro: Farragut West

Opening times
Mon, Wed, Fri to Sun 10–5. Thur 10–9. Closed Tue, Christmas and New Years Day

Entrance fee
Suggested donation: $3.00

Tours
Guided tours daily at 12.30 and 7.30 on Thursday

La Bacchante au Tambourin

1860

Jean-Baptiste-Camille Corot

This fine classical odalisque in a verdant landscape is a good example of Corot's (1796–1875) later work. The landscape is peopled by bacchanalian revellers and the odalisque reclines with a tambourine in her hand. Although this is only one of a number of Corots' works in the collection, it is a masterpiece showing a successful marriage between the realist and Neoclassical styles that were prevalent in mid nineteenth-century French art, although in many ways these were in conflict. The odalisque is a mythical nude from Arcadia transported to the forest of Barbizon. She may be based on a nude study entitled *Marietta* that Corot had made in Rome in 1843, yet there is no doubt that Corot had the example of Ingres' odalisques in mind when he painted her.

It was at this time in the mid 1860s that Corot changed his painting style from the robust direct vision of nature seen in his early work and replaced it with a somewhat artificial landscape style incorporating wafting foliage and allusions to Classical subjects. In contrast to his fresh open air paintings this is very much a studio work.

The Ballet School

c. 1873

Edgar Degas

Like his fellow Impressionist Monet, Degas (1834–1917) liked to return to the same subjects again and again in his art. Perhaps the most popular of these recurrent themes was ballet dancers and the ballet school. This is an exceptional example of the genre, both for its colour and the wonderful manipulation of light and space. Ever the formal perfectionist despite his choice of contemporary themes, Degas was influenced by photography, and his compositions are conceived as though they fall within a photographic frame. In this painting the spectator is introduced to the strong diagonal from top left to bottom right through the ballet dancers descending the spiral staircase. Only their legs can be seen, but this gives us the impression of a space beyond, and Degas has subtly arranged his figures in groups that lead the eye through the relative gloom of the main room through to the interior in the distance, which is lit by strong natural light. In order to balance the composition Degas has brought into play colour highlights in the pink and red bows, ballet shoes and shawls, creating a counter-balancing rhythm. No personalities intrude: faces are turned away from the spectator or are immersed in shadow. It is interesting to contrast this painting with the emotionally charged *Melancholy* in the Phillips Collection (page 109), a work that is wholly different in character.

The Departure

1837

Thomas Cole

This painting and its companion piece *The Return* are two of Cole's most famous works. Although he was born in England, Cole (1801–48) can lay claim to being the first painter of the Hudson River School of American landscape. In the mid 1820s he started exploring the Hudson River Valley and the wilder countryside beyond, and the paintings he produced became immensely popular. His travels though Europe in the 1830s and 1840s led to his producing landscapes with allegorical and moralistic subjects, often conceived in series. This work and its companion were originally commissioned as morning and evening landscapes. A medieval knight is shown setting forth on crusade with his retinue in the morning picture, and in its companion he returns at sunset. Carried home, he is either dead or dying with his mournful companions following behind.

Niagara

1857

Frederick Church

Church (1826–1900) was the only pupil of Thomas Cole and became a major figure of the Hudson River School, whose artists celebrated the might and grandeur of the scenery of America. Niagara was the most famous of America's natural wonders and in the Romantic age when pantheistic ideas of God in nature prevailed, the Falls were seen as a place of great spiritual power. The picture achieved immediate fame after it was painted, and was exhibited both in the United States and England. In its overpowering breadth and large scale, it admirably conveys the immensity of the landscape. Church also employed a subtle compositional device, using a double rainbow with one arc balanced by a secondary arc caused by the light refracting through the spray of the mighty waterfall.

No-one chronicled the life of the American West like Frederic Remington (1861–1909), whose images of cattlemen, Red Indians, settlers and gun-fighters are as much an archetype as John Wayne, and a good deal more authentic. Like George Catlin before him, Remington portrayed a society and way of life that was soon to pass into legend. Born in upstate New York and educated at Yale, he first travelled West when he was nineteen in the summer of 1881. From this visit he acquired a taste for the landscape and those who populated it. He began his career as an illustrator for popular journals such as *Harpers Weekly* and *Century* magazine. As well as being a popular illustrator, he sought recognition as a fine artist, initially exhibiting paintings and, later on, bronze sculpture.

This bronze group, also entitled *Coming through the Rye*, was copyrighted in 1902 and was the most ambitious sculpture Remington had executed to that date. It is now one of his most popular works, showing old time cowboys of the northern plains whooping it up and firing into the air with their six guns. More than forty original bronzes were cast and Tiffany and Co. of New York sold them for $2000 each.

When Remington died in 1909 at the young age of forty-eight, President Theodore Roosevelt wrote: 'the soldier, the cowboy and rancher, the Indian, the horse and the cattle of the plains will live in his pictures, I verily believe, for all time.'

Built 1799

Address
2715, Q Street, NW,
Washington D.C. 20007
✆ (202) 337 2288

Map reference
⑤

How to get there
Metro: Dupont Circle
D.C. Bus: D2, D4, D6, D8

Opening times
Tue to Sat 10–1. Closed
Sun, Mon, Federal holidays
and the week between
Christmas and New Year

Entrance fee
Adults $3, seniors $2.50,
groups $2.50. Children
under 18 free

Tours
Compulsory guided tours

Dumbarton House is the national headquarters of the National Society for the Colonial Dames of America. One of the finest houses in Georgetown, it was built in 1799 as a Federal style red brick mansion with an imposing portico and additional limestone quoins. The rooms are furnished with Sheraton and Hepplewhite style pieces from the Federal period, from Philadelphia and New York. The house also boasts a good collection of crystal and china. There is a notable portrait by Charles Wilson Peale of the children of Benjamin Stoddert which has as its background a view of Georgetown and the Potomac as it appeared in 1789.

One can happily combine a visit to both Dumbarton House and the nearby Tudor Place (page 121) with a general walk around Georgetown to view the superb Federal architecture. Although it had declined in importance by the 1820s, Georgetown then became one of the most pleasant places to live in Washington. Since 1950 it has been designated a national historic district and many of the older buildings have been refurbished.

Set in a delightful garden which is open to the public, Dumbarton Oaks is a Federal mansion enlarged in the nineteenth century, which was acquired in 1920 by Mr. and Mrs. Robert Woods Bliss. Both were independently wealthy and outstanding collectors, an activity to which they devoted all their time after Mr. Bliss retired from the Diplomatic Corps in 1933. Their interests although various were mainly concentrated on Byzantine and Pre-Columbian art, and it is in these areas that the glory of the collection lies. The museum, house and grounds are now the property of Harvard University, to whom they were donated in 1940.

The gallery space is divided into three main sections. The area housing the Byzantine works was added in 1940, and contains some mosaic flooring as well as cabinets for the major exhibits. There is a central court area with adjoining rooms for antique and Byzantine treasures. The Music Room, where amongst others the great pianist and statesman Jan Paderewski performed, was added in 1929 and contains a sixteenth-century stone chimney piece. It is furnished with French, Spanish and Italian furniture from the sixteenth and seventeenth centuries. *The Visitation* by El Greco also hangs here. In 1938 on the Bliss's thirtieth wedding anniversary, Igor Stravinsky performed his concerto in E flat here. Commissioned for the occasion, it has since been known as the Dumbarton Oaks concerto. In 1944 the Music Room housed two international meetings known as the Dumbarton Oaks Conferences. These formulated the basis for the charter of the United Nations, which was created the following year.

The Pre-Columbian exhibition section was completed in 1963. Designed by the celebrated architect Philip Johnson, it is a small though exquisite series of eight circular linked buildings arranged in formation around a circular fountain court of the same size.

Address
1703 32nd St NW,
Washington D.C.
✆ (202) 338 8278

Map reference

How to get there
Bus: Take any 30s bus to Wisconsin Avenue and R St and then walk one block east on R Street.

Opening times
Gallery: Tue to Sun 2–5. Closed Mon and Federal holidays
Garden: Daily 2–5

Entrance fee
$1 contribution required

Hellenistic Horse

Second or third century AD

This magnificent rearing horse was probably originally one of a pair of equestrian statues, possibly flanking the entrance to a temple. There is an inscription engraved on the horse's left shoulder which mentions the offering of two horses and their riders by the chief of a local tribe, and the lettering suggests a date around the second century AD. The horse was found in Yemen and was reconstructed from over eighty fragments. The tail is missing as are some other important areas. It would appear that there were originally pieces of a bit and bridle in the mouth, and despite the amazing restoration work there are some rather irregular aspects to the pose. It is, however, a wonderful work and as a prize piece, it is located in the middle of the main hall of the antiquities collection.

This part of the gallery is divided between works which were created under the Byzantine Empire and others, which like the horse, belong to a previous epoch and are geographically outside its ambit. Among the other highlights of the Bliss's collection of antique and Byzantine art are the sixth-century Syrian floor mosaics, the incomparable assemblage of over 21,000 Byzantine coins, the Egyptian Coptic textiles and a wonderful collection of Byzantine ivories, vestments and ecclesiatical plate.

This marvel of the art of mosaic was probably executed in Constantinople early in the fourteenth century, during the late flowering of Byzantine culture known as the Paleologan renaissance. This is one of the latest of all the Byzantine works in the collection, and depicts forty Roman soldiers who were left to die in a frozen lake because they were Christians. According to the legend a warm bath house was set up on the shore for those who would deny their faith. Only one of the forty recanted and he was replaced by the guardian of the bathhouse who converted to Christianity on seeing the weak soul disappear in a puff of smoke. The martyrs are seen shivering in the foreground, their feet in the water. Behind is a gold background and at the top of the panel the arc of heaven is depicted with the hand of God. Other details have sadly been lost.

This miniature mosaic style thrived in the latter years of the Byzantine Empire, but because of the fragility of the wax ground into which the minute tesserae are placed very few examples have survived. The tesserae are made of enamelled paste, semi-precious stones and precious metals. The delicacy of the rather painterly mosaic technique is not dissimilar to the style of icon painting which was so popular at the time.

Roberts Woods Bliss was one of the first connoisseurs in the United States to devote his attention to the art of Central and South America up to the time of the Spanish invasions. He started acquiring works in 1914 and amassed a superb collection representing a range of pre-Columbian cultures which are now arranged in separate glass pavilions. There can be no doubt that his collection was highly influential in the acceptance of indigenous American artefacts as fine art rather than simply items of ethnographic interest.

A very strong section is that representing the Aztec culture of Mexico. This mottled grey stone mask sculpture represents Tezcatlipoca, the supreme deity of the Aztec pantheon. He was usually associated with rulership, the night and divination. The mask, with added ear ornaments, may have portrayed the face of his cult image, but is not a true mask as there are no eye holes. The carving in general is unusually delicate and shows details of the bone structure and headdress. On the reverse side the year 'two rood' or 1507 is recorded, marking the last cyclical ceremony celebrated by the Aztecs, who divided time into fifty-two-year periods which correspond in concept to our centuries.

The Freer Gallery was the first museum devoted to art to be opened on the Mall under the auspices of the Smithsonian. In his endowment, Freer made it clear that the Gallery was for 'the encouragement of the study of the civilizations of the Far East.'

Charles Lang Freer was born in Kingston, New York, in 1854 of humble parentage. He left school at the age of fourteen to work in a cement factory, later becoming an accountant for the local railway before embarking on a business career, manufacturing railroad cars in Detroit. This was to make him one of the richest men in the USA. At the age of forty-six, Freer retired from business in order to devote his time to collecting. He made four visits to Asia, purchasing work from China, Japan, Korea, India, Southeast Asia and Iran.

At its opening in 1923, the neo-Renaissance style gallery building contained 2500 items, but these have been vastly increased both by later purchases by Freer himself, and by the museum's acquisition of many extra works of art. Freer was anxious to promote contemporary American art. It was a liking for the work of Whistler which did most to kindle his enthusiasm, and it was no doubt their mutual enthusiasm for Asian art which attracted the two personalities to one another. Whistler did a great deal to shape Freer's taste in both Oriental and Occidental art. Among Freer's collection is one of Whistler's most oriental paintings, *The Golden Screen* (page 11). Other American painters collected by the donor were Sargent, Tryon, Dewing and Thayer.

The building is linked to the Arthur M. Sackler Gallery (page 116) by an underground passage exhibition space. Owing to the similarity of their collections there is a great deal of interaction between the two museums, both of which rotate their holdings.

Address
Jefferson Drive and 12th St SW. Washington D.C.
 (202) 357 2700

Map reference
⑦

How to get there
Metro: Smithsonian

Opening times
Daily 10–5.30. Closed Christmas Day

Entrance fee
Free entrance

Tours
Daily tour schedules are listed in the calender of events and at the information desk

1876–77

James Abbott McNeill Whistler

The Peacock Room has a bizarre and interesting history. One of Whistler's (1834–1903) patrons, a Liverpool shipping magnate by the name of F.W. Leyland, decided that he wanted to have a London residence that fulfilled his fantasy of being a sixteenth-century Venetian merchant in modern London. Having bought his house, he began redecorating the interior. One of the rooms was to contain his fine collection of blue and white Chinese porcelain, and a painting by Whistler called *La Princesse dans le Pays de Porcelain*. The walls were to be covered with Spanish leather and decorated with flowers and pomegranates. Whistler objected to the leather against which his painting was to be hung and asked Leyland if he could lighten the surface with some patches of yellow.

Leyland consented to this request, but Whistler then decided to change the whole decor without asking further permission. He painted all the leather in a deep Prussian blue and then added the golden birds. Leyland was away from London for the whole period of the decoration and completion, and on his return he was so horrified with the transformation he refused to pay the artist the £2000 fee he demanded. Whistler, who was on the verge of bankrupcy, was obliged to accept the £1000 which Leyland paid to get rid of him. The two were thereafter bitter enemies. Charles Freer bought the *Princesse* painting in 1903 and added the full Peacock Room to his collection a year later.

Breakfast in the Loggia

1910

John Singer Sargent

By the time he produced this delightful work, Sargent (1856–1925) was well over fifty and one of the most popular portrait painters in Europe and America. Here is a painting executed with obvious pleasure, depicting two of the artist's friends, Eliza Wedgwood and Jane Emmet de Glehn, at the Villa Torre Galli outside Florence. The sunlight filtering through the trees into the elegant loggia animates the whole scene with a myriad of colours playing upon a multitude of objects. Sargent himself was very familiar with this kind of environment. He was born in Florence to American parents, and fraternized with the most cultivated members of European society. With its air of refinement, the Tuscan morning conversation reads like a passage from a novel by Sargent's friend, Henry James.

Japanese Demon Guardians of the Temple

Thirteenth century AD

The Freer has an extensive collection of Japanese art covering not only sculpture but also lacquerwork, paintings and ceramics. These guardian figures or *Nio* are of a type that would have been placed at the entrance gateways to the walled compounds of Buddhist temple complexes. Their exaggerated and distorted musculature gives the demons a terrible superhuman aspect designed to fend off evil. Such guardian figures were said to have followed and protected the Buddha when he travelled through India. The figures are well over life-size and were probably originally placed in open alcoves at the Temple of Lehara Dera in Sakai near Osaka, Japan, which would account for their weathering. They are made of numerous wooden blocks cleverly shaped and then fixed together with wooden pegs, iron staples and glue.

Bronze Figure of Goddess Parvati
Tenth century AD

Chola bronzes are some of the most appealing and accomplished of all Indian sculptures and are a highly characteristic product of the Dravidian peoples of South India. Five hundred years before Donatello was working in Florence, the Chola civilization was producing these elegant bronze figures using the lost wax process. In all these castings only one figure was ever produced as the mould was destroyed after the first casting. The image of the god or goddess would be kept in a temple storehouse for most of the year and brought out for religious processions in honour of the deity.

This is an image of the goddess Parvati, consort of the god Siva. She is one manifestation of the *devi* or feminine force in the Universe, and here she is an elegant and beautiful woman. What makes this image somewhat unique is the fact that she has the features of Sembiyan Mahadevi, a Queen of the Chola dynasty, and yet she conforms to the strict canons of representation laid out in the *Shulpa Shastras*, the manuals dictating the laws of proportion and iconography in the visual arts. The subtle elegance of this sensuous figure is exquisite. The grace of her hips and breasts, her languid pose and manner in which the crown, jewellery and garment melt into the form of the body, display supreme accomplishment and provide an uninterrupted rhythm through the lines and contours of the deity.

This fine example of Mughal manuscript painting comes from the hand of Abu'l Hasan who was so admired by his patron, the Emperor Jahangir, that he had the title 'Nadir al Zaman', or 'Wonder of the Age' bestowed upon him. The Imperial court was highly cultivated and Jahangir himself, the fourth of the great Mughal Emperors, was a supreme enthusiast and connoisseur.

The iconography and treatment of this painting are of great interest. Jahangir recorded that he had a dream in which his enemy, Shah Abbas Safavi of Persia, appeared in a well of light and made him happy. Abbas was at that time engaged in a war with Jahangir over possessions in what is now Afganistan. The Indian ruler was not in a good position in this conflict and eventually lost some of his territory there. No doubt in order to boost his patron's confidence, the artist depicted a towering Emperor standing atop a lion whereas the rather diminutive Shah is embraced whilst treading on a symbolic sheep. Both these figures are placed on an image of the globe.

The various influences which combined to form the Mughal style of miniature illumination can be seen in this painting. Although their work was based on Persian models, the illuminators of the Mughal court absorbed some aspects of the indigenous Indian tradition. They were also acutely aware of European painting styles, and this work, with its winged cherubs and European cartography, illustrates this influence.

Built c. 1750

Address
Mason Neck, Virginia
22079
✆ (703) 550 9220

Map reference
⑧

How to get there
From Mount Vernon follow
the signs on Route 1 south.

Opening times
House: daily 9.30–5.
Grounds: daily 9.30–6.
Closed Thanksgiving,
Christmas, New Years Day

Entrance fee
Adults $5, seniors $4,
children under 18 $1.50

Tours
Tours available every half
hour

This small but eminently charming manor house
was the home of George Mason, one of the
wealthiest landowners of eighteenth-century
Virginia and a founding father of the United
States. Mason was the author of the Virginia
Declaration of Rights, a prototype for the
Declaration of Independence and the Bill of
Rights as attached to the Constitution of the
United States.

The unostentatious mansion – typical of the
modest home of a patrician plantation owner –
is set in a beautiful wooded park and garden
with views over the Potomac. All the furnishings
and objets d'art are from the Colonial and
Federal periods. Some of the furnishings were
brought from England and some manufactured
in the colonies. There is also some fine stucco-
work, notably in the Chinese dining room, which
unique in North America.

The house has a small museum with a video
show and exhibits associated with George Mason
and his family. There is also a small schoolhouse
in the garden, with desks and canes to adminis-
ter punishment.

Situated in a pleasant north Washington suburb, Hillwood was the estate of Margaret Merriweather Post, one of the wealthiest women of her age and an outstanding collector. The house still has the feel of a private residence even though today it constitutes the finest museum of the decorative arts of Russia outside the former Soviet Union. It took a combination of fortunate circumstances and a very perceptive collector to amass this notable assembly of artefacts.

Margaret Merriweather Post was born in 1887, the only child of cereals magnate Charles William Post, who at an early age encouraged his daughter to start collecting as an activity befitting an heiress of her stature. She began by collecting French eighteenth-century porcelain and furniture. Her third marriage in 1935 to Washington lawyer Joseph E Davies took her to Moscow when her husband became ambassador to the Soviet Union in 1937. It was at this time that the impoverished Soviet government was selling art which had been confiscated from the former Imperial family, aristocracy and church. As one of the last foreigners to be able to acquire these works of art, Margaret Post formed the nucleus of her Russian collection there, while establishing her enthusiasm for the art of that country. She carried on collecting Russian art for the rest of her life, once remarking that she had acquired Russian objects in eleven different countries.

Originally built in the 1920s, Hillwood was purchased and remodelled by Mrs. Post in 1955. She also laid out the magnificent garden which contains a traditional Dacha, or Russian summer house. Visitors are shown a film illustrating the life of Mrs. Post, and then given a detailed and well-informed guided tour of the house.

Address
4155, Linnaean Avenue NW
Washington D.C. 20008
☎ (202) 686 5807

Map reference

How to get there
Metro: Van Ness then one mile walk.
Bus: L1 or L2 along Connecticut Avenue to Tilden Street. Thereafter a half-mile walk

Opening times
Tue to Sat 9–3. Closed Sun, Mon

Entrance fee
Adults $10; students $5. Children under 12 not admitted

Tours
Compulsory tours at 9, 10.30, 12, 1.30 and 3 Reservations required, recommended at least one week in advance

The Buch Chalice

1791

This fabulously ornate chalice was commissioned by Catherine the Great in 1790 to place in the St. Alexander Nevski Monastery in St. Petersburg. It was made by the celebrated goldsmith Ivor Wenfeldt Buch, a Norwegian-born Dane who emigrated to St. Petersburg and became one of the most celebrated goldsmiths at court while at the same time serving as the Danish Consul. The thirteen-inch high chalice is inlaid with diamonds and carved stones with gold wheat and fruit on the stem. Around the bowl are four exquisitely carved oval stones depicting three scenes from the Passion of Christ and one showing the Archangel Michael. It is inscribed on the base in French *Fabriqué de Buch a St Petersbourg Ao 1791*.

Outstanding though this work is, it is just one of numerous items of high artistic quality and value at Hillwood. Lovers of icons, enamelwork, glassware, Fabergé eggs, jewellery and porcelain will find much in the museum to draw their attention. There are fine Russian pieces of furniture from the Imperial period and a number of paintings, with a particular emphasis on portraits of Catherine the Great, her household and family.

Joseph Hirshhorn was a Latvian immigrant who made a vast fortune as a financier and uranium magnate. As his taste for academic paintings gave way to contemporary art, he acquired the reputation of being the most dynamic collector in New York. His acquisitiveness seemed to know no bounds and he filled his offices and residences with sculpture and paintings to the point of overflowing. By the 1960s this collection had achieved an international reputation, inspiring the British Government's offer to establish a museum for the collection in London. This was followed by similar offers from numerous other cities. Late in 1964, Hirshhorn was persuaded to present his collection to the USA under the aegis of the Smithsonian Institution. A site on the Mall was selected, and in 1966 the necessary legislation establishing the museum passed through Congress.

The radical building, designed by Gordon Bunshaft, resembles a massive ring resting on four giant concrete piers enclosing a central courtyard with fountain. The exhibition area is divided into two: an inner ring for sculpture lit by large floor-to-ceiling windows, and an outer ring which is largely devoted to the exhibition of paintings. The plaza around the building and the adjacent sculpture garden are used to exhibit the more monumental sculptural pieces.

Only about 900 of over 12,000 items in the collection can be shown at any one time. Apart from the works in the sculpture garden the collection is circulated regularly, but the museum always shows a representative selection of its holdings.

Address
Independence Avenue and 7th St SW, Washington D.C.
✆ (202) 357 2700

Map reference

How to get there
Metro: L'Enfant Plaza or Smithsonian

Opening times
Museum: daily 10–5.30. Sculpture garden: daily 7.30–dusk. Closed Christmas Day

Entrance fee
Free entrance

Tours
Daily at 10.30, 12, 1.30 and 2.30. Sundays at 12.30

Doves
(first version)

1913

Jacob Epstein

A central figure in the history of British sculpture, Epstein (1880–1959) is perhaps best known for his monumental religious sculptures and celebrated portraits. This work, however, comes from his early and most original period. From 1911 he became associated with a group of radical young British artists headed by Wyndham Lewis, who called themselves the Vorticists. Epstein himself produced the great icon of Vorticist art, a robotic expression of mechanical power entitled *Rock Drill*. At the same time he was working on this sculpture, the subtle tranquillity and stylized simplicity of which contrasted with his violent Futurist-inspired figures. He was radically influenced by his contemporaries Modigliani and Brancusi and was himself a great influence on Gaudier-Brzeska.

Alexandre Dumas Fils

1873

Jean-Baptiste Carpeaux

Although it remained traditional in terms of subject matter and format, Carpeaux's sculpture broke free of convention to became both expressive and sensitive in a manner which was revolutionary for his period. Carpeaux (1827–75) infused his figures with an animation that few, if any, other sculptors of the European tradition have been able to equal, truthfully conveying physical appearances while passionately reflecting life's pleasure and pain as a true artist of the Romantic tradition. These elements can be seen in this lively portrait bust of the author of *La Dame aux Camelias*, a noted dandy and one of the greatest literary figures of his day. Carpeaux's influence as a painter and sculptor was far reaching. His painting style inspired the Impressionists, and in sculpture his leading pupil was Auguste Rodin.

Rodin (1840–1917) was possibly the greatest and certainly one of the most influential sculptors of the nineteenth century. *The Burghers of Calais*, which exists in several castings, is one of his great masterpieces.

In 1884 when Rodin was forty-four, the city of Calais opened a competition for a monument to the memory of Eustace de Saint Pierre, the burgher who had delivered the keys of the city to Edward III of England in 1347, following an eleven-month siege. Instead of the single figure, Rodin showed six burghers of the town with their hands bound, clad in sackcloth, sacrificing themselves for the sake of the safe deliverance of their city. The work met with savage criticism when it was finally completed and delivered in 1895. Members of the city council of Calais argued that the burghers had not been depicted as sufficiently heroic. Rodin had laboured ten hard years studying the personalities of the individuals in their various poses expressive of grief and despair, while also trying to convey the nobler virtues of civic duty.

All the elements of Rodin's style are present here: his understanding of human anatomy; the violent plasticity of the bronze; and the powerful expression seen in the heads of the major figures. Located in the sculpture garden, this is the largest and most famous of the many works by Rodin in the collection.

Wrestler

1912

Henri Gaudier-Brzeska

This small but impressive sculpture is the work of yet another artist of rare talent whose life was tragically cut short by World War One: he was killed in action in 1914 after joining the French army. Although he was born in France, Gaudier-Brzeska (1891–1915) commenced his artistic education in England and then moved to Germany. Returning to England, he became associated with the Vorticist group led by Wyndham Lewis. As well as being a sculptor, Gaudier-Bzeska was also a fine draughtsman, producing some excellent drawings of animals. The robust strength expressed in this male nude is similar in character to other works by the Vorticists, notably the paintings of William Roberts. Jacob Epstein had a significant influence on his work as a sculptor.

Head

C. 1911–12

Amedeo Modigliani

When the Italian artist Modigliani (1884–1920) arrived in Paris in 1906, he was highly influenced by Picasso and his circle, and it was in this environment that he developed his idiosyncratic, linear style. Whether it was through Picasso or through direct contact with African sculptures, there can be no doubting the influence of tribal art on Modigliani's simplified and elongated bodies and faces. This influence can also be seen in the painting entitled *Gypsy Girl* from the National Gallery of Art reproduced on page 12. In the sculpture illustrated above we have a genuinely primitive image; features are roughly hewn from the rock with all the directness that we see in the best tribal art. It is interesting to compare this image with the mask from the National Museum of African Art (page 93).

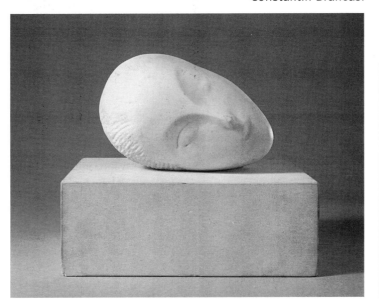

It is difficult to over-estimate the importance of Brancusi (1876–1957) for twentieth-century sculpture, for he is one of the supreme masters of the medium. A Rumanian by birth, he moved to Paris in 1904 where he studied sculpture and began exhibiting, remaining there until his death.

As his style developed he became more and more concerned with abstract shape, or rather, abstracted representational forms. His highly polished sculpted heads, birds and fish are arguably his most successful works. He was concerned that sculpture should abandon academic traditions and return to extreme simplicity of form.

Starting in 1906 Brancusi, who loved developing specific themes, began sculpting a series of heads in which physical features were reduced so that all concentration was on the pure form of the head. This marble piece is a radical manifestation of this simplification. Facial features have been minimalised, leaving only a subtle suggestion of eyes, nose, mouth and hair. Like an anthropomorphic egg, the entire meaning of the work has been absorbed into a single orb-like shape.

Perhaps appropriate to this sculpture is Brancusi's statement written many years later that: 'Simplicity is not an end in art, but one arrives at simplicity in spite of oneself, in approaching the real sense of things. Simplicity is at bottom complexity and one must be nourished in its essence to understand its significance.'

Eiffel Tower

1924–26

Robert Delaunay

Robert Delaunay's (1885–1941) contribution to modern painting is often under-estimated. His own interpretation of Cubism brought into play the emotional effects engendered by pure colour, and this dual preoccupation with colour and abstract form not only links his work with the German Expressionists but also gave the style invented by Picasso and Braque an added dimension. With his wife Sonia, Robert Delaunay created a style which came to be known as Orphic Cubism.

The Eiffel Tower is a recurring theme in Delaunay's work, and it became the reference point for his painterly experiments. For him it was the master symbol of modern culture which could be portrayed as a quasi-abstract image, but which was always an identifiable, familiar object however much it was distorted on canvas. Delaunay started painting the Tower in 1909 after he had left the main group of Cubists. In the work of this early period the Tower often appears to crumble in multiple forms seen through refracted light. This picture, however, belongs to a later period and the treatment is quite different. Having spent World War One in Spain and Portugal, the Delaunays returned to Paris and Robert readopted the Eiffel Tower as a subject for his art. In this example it is seen from the air, with the curves of the Champ de Mars and the grid of the street appearing as a patchwork below. In this work the motif just emerges from what is otherwise a pure abstract pattern of dynamic, pulsating colours.

Golden Days

1944–49

Balthus (Balthasar Klossowski de Rola)

From the time of his arrival in Paris in the 1920s, the enigmatic Polish painter Balthus (b. 1908) established his own idiosyncratic style from which he has deviated very little, concentrating on expressing the same mood and working with the same subject matter. His primary concern is with awakening sexual awareness in adolescent girls. In this work the girl reclines on a sofa, one leg raised as she stares into a mirror. In the background a blazing fire is being tended by a figure immersed in shadow. The focus is on the girl, the narcissism of youth, and the self-consciousness of adolescence. The doll-like quality of the figures give Balthus's work the feeling of being one step removed from reality.

The Dog

1951

Alberto Giacometti

One of the most important sculptors of the century, the Swiss-born Giacometti (1901–66) is best known for his figures of elongated human figures with diminutive heads and gaunt wiry bodies. With their knobbly ravaged skin they are highly expressive, not least because of the immense feeling of space they generate around them. The figures often appear lonely, isolated, and perhaps suffering. It is this sense that Giacometti wanted to express in the sculpture of *The Dog*. 'I am the dog' he remarked when asked to comment on the sculpture. Perhaps he felt that he himself was dejected and abused like the emaciated creature. It is perhaps significant that he was working in Paris in the 1940s and 1950s, for his work has been perceptively described as the visual manifestation of existential man.

King and Queen

1952–53

Henry Moore

Joseph Hirshhorn was an avid collector with wide-ranging tastes in both two- and three-dimensional art. One artist whose work he was particularly enthusiastic about was the British sculptor, Henry Moore (1898–1986). He acquired his first Moore in 1951 and carried on adding further pieces to the collection almost every year until his death.

This bronze group is one of an edition originally commissioned by the town of Antwerp for their Middleheim Sculpture Garden. Moore wrote about the sculpture: 'Anything can start me off on a sculpture idea, and in this case it was playing with a small piece of modelling wax. Whilst manipulating a piece of wax, it began to look like a horned, pan-like bearded head. Then it grew a crown and I recognized it immediately as the head of a King. I continued and gave it a body. When wax hardens, it is almost as strong as metal. I used this special strength to repeat in the body the aristocratic refinement I found in the head. Then I added the second figure to it and it became a King and Queen'. He continued: 'I realize now that it was because I was reading stories to Mary, my six-year-old daughter, every night and most of them were about kings and queens and princesses.'

The newest museum in Washington, this is not really an art museum at all since it is devoted to the presentation of the history of Jewish and other victims of Nazi persecution from 1933 to 1945, the origins and consequences of the Holocaust. From an artistic point of view it is the building which is of most interest, but as this is an excellent historical museum dealing with the most profound of human tragedies, it should be visited by anyone spending time in Washington.

The brief for the design of the building as stipulated by the United States Holocaust Memorial Council was to provide a museum of 'symbolic and artistic beauty that is visually and emotionally moving in accordance with the solemn nature of the Holocaust.' James I. Freed of Pei Cobb Freed and Partners of New York developed the design of the building, which is visually exciting both inside and out. One cannot avoid, however, thinking about prisons and concentration camps as there are stark references in the architecture which implicitly remind one of such horrors. This is particularly so in the large atrium Hall of Remembrance conceived as the memorial to the six million who died as a result of the Holocaust. The brutal concrete walls and steel beams with open corridors above have a feeling both of prison and of factory.

The building has five floors of exhibition space, including two auditoria, a special children's section and three floors of permanent exhibition tracing the history and consequences of the Holocaust from 1933 to the present day. There is also a sophisticated computer-based learning facility and an extensive library.

Address
14 Independence Avenue SW, Washington D.C.
✆ (202) 488 0400

Map reference

How to get there
Metro: Smithsonian
Tourmobile also visits the museum

Opening times
Daily 10–5.30

Entrance fee
Free entrance

Jefferson Memorial

Built 1934–43

Address
Tidal basin, West Potomac Park, Washington D.C.
✆ (202) 426 6822

Map reference

How to get there
Metro: Smithsonian. On the tourmobile route

Opening times
Daily 8am–midnight. Closed Christmas Day

Entrance fee
Free entrance

Tours
Guided tours on request

This controversial monument was only authorized by Congress in 1934, over one hundred years after the death of Thomas Jefferson, the third President and author of the Declaration of Independence. It was designed by John Russell Pope, the architect of the National Gallery of Art, and the appearance of the building, derived from the Pantheon in Rome, follows the austere and unpretentious classical style for which Pope was famous. An Ionic colonnade encircles the open interior space, which is dominated by a bronze statue of Jefferson by Rudolph Evans. The walls are inscribed with the words of the brilliant statesman and thinker. The exterior pediment has a relief of Jefferson surrounded by the other individuals chosen to draft the Declaration of Independence. Although constructed to only half the size of its original design, the building works well as a monument, not least because it is located on an axis line with the White House and the Washington monument, consistent with the L'Enfant's original town planning concept.

Washington's newest museum opened its doors to the public on 1 June 1994. It is a wonderful addition to the already bountiful array of art collections in the capital. Designed by Phillip Johnson in 1967, the building was the home of David and Carmen Kreeger, and is set in five-and-a-half acres of woodland. It was designed both with the art collection in mind and to provide space for musical performances. David Kreeger was an accomplished musician and he invited many famous performers to play in the Great Hall, which has outstanding accoustics.

David Kreeger, who came to Washington in the 1930s as a New Deal lawyer, made his fortune through the GEICO insurance concern and used much of his wealth in the collection and patronage of the arts. Over 180 works of art are displayed in the museum. These are mostly nineteenth- and twentieth-century European paintings and sculpture, but there are also examples of African and South Asian art. The collection has a personal quality similar to that of the Phillips Collection. Among the Impressionists and Post-Impressionists are works by Renoir and Monet, Van Gogh, Cézanne, Bonnard and Modigliani. Modern art movements are represented by a fine range of paintings from Picasso and Braque through to the Expressionists, Surrealists such as Kandinsky and Man Ray, to the abstract works of the New York School by artists such as Hans Hoffman and Clyfford Still. Among the sculptures are works by Henry Moore, David Smith, Brancusi, Rodin and Maillol.

Address
2401 Foxhall Road NW,
Washington D.C.
© (202) 338 3552

Map reference

How to get there
No metro lines or bus lines are located near the Museum. Taxis are advised

Opening times
Tue to Sat at tour times listed below. Closed Sun, Mon and Federal holidays

Entrance fee
Suggested donation $5. Children over 12 welcomed

Tours
Compulsory guided tours lasting one and a half hours daily at 10.30 and 1.30. Reservations necessary. Call (202) 338 3552. Group tours also available if booked in advance

Address
101 First St SE, Washington
D.C.
✆ (202) 707 5000

Map reference
⑭

How to get there
Metro: Capitol South or
Union Station

Opening times
Closed until 1997. Normally
Exhibition Halls: Mon to Fri
8.30–9.30; Sat 8.30–6;
Closed Sun and Federal
holidays

Entrance fee
Free entrance

Tours
Phone for information on
guided tours

–

Today the largest library in the world, the Library of Congress was founded at the beginning of the nineteenth century. In 1800 while the Congress was still convening in Philadelphia, it voted $5000 for the establishment of a library for its own use. The original three thousand volumes of this library were destroyed by the British in 1814 when they burned the Capitol building. In response to this, ex-President Jefferson offered his library of some six-and-a-half thousand volumes to the nation for $23,950. Another fire destroyed much of this, in 1851, and in response Congress made funds available for the building of a separate library area on the west side of the Capitol. Gradually the Library became a public institution, the National Library of the United States. It was also able to obtain the copyright on all publications in the USA and this continuing practice substantially increased its holding. A building devoted exclusively to the Library was erected but was only completed in 1897. Known as the Thomas Jefferson Building, it contains the main reading room with its impressive central dome. Two extra buildings have been added this century, the John Adams Building and the James Madison Memorial Building in 1939 and 1980 respectively.

The library contains some ninety million items including many famous manuscripts such as the Bible of Mainz and a Gutenberg Bible. There are also American manuscripts of importance such as Jefferson's first draft of the Declaration of Independence, and hand-written drafts of the Gettysburg Address and Emancipation Proclamations. The collection of musical manuscripts and objects is also justly famous. The main reading room can be visited on application to the visitors information desk in the James Madison Building, where there are always displayed a number of exhibits from the Library's special collections.

The monumental classical temple housing Lincoln's memorial provides a fitting conclusion to the east–west axis of the Mall. Set in front of a long reflecting pool, vistas of the monument are very dramatic and beautiful, and it is one of the great sights of Washington when illuminated at night.

The monument was proposed very shortly after Lincoln's untimely assassination, but it was not until the early years of this century that decisions were made on its location and design. The architect, Henry Bacon, adopted the Doric style with large entablature and thirty-six columns to symbolize the number of states in the Union at the time of Lincoln's death. On the exterior frieze are the names of the forty-eight states that existed at the time the monument was built. The twenty-foot high statue of Lincoln in the interior is by Daniel Chester French. Also within the interior are inscriptions taken from the President's second inaugural speech and the Gettysberg Address, and reliefs depicting the freeing of the slaves and the union of North and South.

Address
West End Of Mall
Washington D.C.
 (202) 426 6895.

Map reference
(15)

How to get there
Metro: Foggy Bottom or
Arlington Cemetery

Opening times
Daily 8–Midnight. Closed
Christmas Day

Entrance fee
Free entrance

Tours
Guided tour available of the
crypt

THE LYCEUM (ALEXANDRIA)
Built 1834

Address
201 S. Washington Street,
Alexandria, VA
✆ (703) 838 4994

Map reference

How to get there
By public transportation:
Metro to King Street Station
and then eastbound Dash
Bus No AT2 or AT5 to
Alexandria. By car: leave
Washington by 14th Street
Bridge and continue south

Opening times
Daily 10–5. Sun 1–5. Closed
Thanksgiving, Christmas
Day, New Years Day

Entrance fee
Free entrance

This impressive Doric building was constructed in 1834 as a cultural centre housing a library, lecture rooms and an exhibition gallery. Since 1974, when it was restored, it has been used as a museum of local art and history with changing exhibitions. The Lyceum is a suitable focus for a visit to Alexandria, which is one of the most unspoiled and charming towns in the United States. Founded in 1749, over the following half century it grew into a prosperous trading port and during that time numerous fine merchants' houses, taverns and churches were built. Any visit to Alexandria should begin at the Ramsay House, which acts as a visitors centre, providing brochures, maps and information on the town and surrounding area. Christ Church, on the corner of North Washington and Cameron Streets, is a fine colonial interpretation of an English Palladian spired church. The grandest residence in Alexandria is the elegant Carlyle House at 121 North Fairfax Street, built of stone in an austere Palladian style. Also worth mentioning is Gadsby's Tavern, a celebrated hostelry since the eighteenth century.

MOUNT VERNON ⭐

Built c. 1735

MOUNT VERNON

Although Mount Vernon is a national shrine, it can also be enjoyed as an elegant Colonial house with a fine double storeyed portico. The tombs of George and Martha Washington are located in the gardens.

George Washington acquired the Mount Vernon estate, some sixteen miles south of Washington, in 1754 when he was twenty-two, and lived there until his death in 1799. His father had built a house on the property around 1735 and this was enlarged and modified both by his brother Lawrence and by George himself. The mansion has been lovingly restored, and the colours of the rooms are those selected by Washington between 1785 and 1799. Fourteen rooms are available for viewing, many of which contain the original furnishings while others have pieces from the Colonial and Federal epochs. It is generally regarded as the finest historic collection in the United States. As well as the furniture and paintings in the house, there is a Mount Vernon Museum in one of the outhouses along the North Lane, which amongst other exhibits contains a portrait bust of George Washington by Houdon.

Address
Mount Vernon House,
Mount Vernon, Virginia.
© (703) 780 2000

Map reference
⑰

How to get there
Metro to Huntington then bus Fairfax connector 101. Tourmobile goes to Mount Vernon daily. By boat: from mid March to October the Spirit of Mount Vernon makes two return trips daily

Opening times
April to Aug daily 8–5. Sept to Mar 9–4

Entrance fee
Adults $7, seniors $6, children 6–11 $3, children under 6 free

53

MUSEUM OF MODERN ART OF LATIN AMERICA

Address
201 18th Sreet NW,
Washington D.C.
✆ (202) 458 6016

Map reference
⑱

How to get there
Metro: Farragut West

Opening times
Tue to Sat 10–5. Closed
Sun, Mon and Federal
holidays

Entrance fee
Free entrance

Tours
Tours of the building can be
arranged with notice

This museum is devoted exclusively to the work of artists from the Caribbean, Central and South America. There is a permanent collection of around 700 items, but most of the rooms are used primarily to exhibit temporary displays of painting and sculpture. The Aztec Garden behind the main building contains sculpture, and is well laid out with architectural motifs reminiscent of the Aztec civilization.

The museum building itself used to serve as the residence of the Secretary General of the Organization of American States, and was only converted into a museum in 1976. Its most notable feature is the stuccoed loggia decorated with Latin American motifs, which looks out on the garden front.

The museum is the visual arts section of the Organization of American States. This international institution was established in 1890 to foster political and economic relations between the independent republics of the American continent. Designed by Paul Cret and Albert Kelsy, the main organization building contains many interesting rooms with original decorative schemes. Outstanding are the Tropical Patio resembling a Spanish colonial courtyard, and the Hall of the Americas, a magnificent space dominated by Tiffany stained glass and chandeliers. English and Spanish guided tours of the Organization building can be arranged with two weeks advance notice

This gallery is not only arguably the finest collection in the United States, but is generally regarded as one of the greatest art museums in the world. The speed with which the collection was assembled and its quality are nothing short of remarkable. It is housed in two buildings on the Mall in Washington known respectively as the West and East Buildings. The former was constructed from 1937 to 1941 at the behest of founder Andrew Mellon, and the latter was opened in 1978 under the auspices of the Trustees. The wedding of the two, though not obvious, has proved a very happy marriage providing an interesting contrast and a range of exhibition spaces in which to view an ever-increasing permanent collection as well as a wide variety of temporary exhibitions. The Neoclassical West Building is the work of John Russell Pope, and generates a grand yet tranquil environment in which to view the works of art. From the exterior the building is homogeneous with the others on the Mall, providing the appropriate classical monumentality in keeping with its situation. Vast Ionic porticoes shelter the main entrances. Inside is the large rotunda and adjoining spacious halls which are designed for the display of monumental sculpture. Beyond these, the internal garden courts provide a verdant and quiet place to rest. Branching off these halls are the rooms which house the permanent collections of painting and sculpture.

The works of art in the West Building are arranged by school following a roughly chronological order, starting with objects from the early Italian Renaissance and terminating with the paintings from late nineteenth-century France. Gallery plans are available, clearly indicating this layout from the information office to the left of the Mall entrance.

Address
West Building: Constitution Avenue and 6th St NW, Washington D.C.
East Building: Constitution Avenue and 4th St NW, Washington D.C.
✆ (202) 737 4215

Map reference

How to get there
Metro: Smithsonian, Archives

Opening times
Mon to Sat 10–5; Sun 11–6.
Closed Christmas Day and New Years Day

Entrance fee
Free entrance

East Building
Built 1978

When it was originally built the West Building appeared more than adequate to house the original bequests and still have room for expansion, but by the 1960s this was certainly not the case, and it was resolved to construct an extra building on an adjoining site. Designed by I.M. Pei, the East Building was opened in 1978. It is built of the same Kentucky marble as the West Building and its sharp angular exterior and flexible interior space have made it a landmark in museum design.

On entry into the building one is impressed by the spacious atrium accommodating a large Calder mobile, a vast tapestry by Miró and several sizeable twentieth-century sculptures by such artists as Anthony Caro and Jean Dubuffet. All the other galleries come off this atrium and their spaces have been designed to be totally flexible, sometimes accommodating highly ambitious temporary exhibitions and at other times a rotation of the works from the permanent collection. The holdings of twentieth-century art are substantial, and only a proportion is ever on display. What is shown, however, is arranged in chronological order and most of the primary individuals and movements in painting, sculpture and the graphic arts are represented. A further and rather unique exhibition space is supplied by the Tower above the main galleries. The galleries are linked below ground by a tunnel passageway which contains a bookshop and cafe as well as a surprising subterranean view of the pyramidal fountains above.

This exquisite small predella panel comes from Duccio's (c. 1255– c. 1318) great masterpiece, the *Maestà*, a vast double-sided altarpiece painted for the Cathedral of Siena, which was completed in 1311. In its simplicity and directness of vision it illustrates some of the finest aspects of Duccio's art. The human interaction is both lucid and poignant. The beckoning gesture of Christ inviting the fishermen to abandon their nets and become 'fishers of men', the powerful look passing between Jesus and Peter, and the figure of Andrew, who is distracted from his task of hauling in the catch, display a wonderfully direct and psychologically intense interpretation of the biblical narrative. Duccio's lack of concern with illusionistic space is shown in the schematized rocky landscape, the elegant boat and abundant sea, all of which resemble theatrical props.

Rooted in the traditions of Byzantine art, Duccio's painting is also infused with influences derived from the Gothic style of Northern European illuminators as well as the nascent humanism then emerging in Central Italy. His wonderful ground colours have retained their intensity and the simple lyricism of his forms, set against a backdrop of gold leaf, beautifully illustrate the sensitive poetry of his style.

When the *Maestà* was completed it was paraded amidst scenes of great festivity from Duccio's workshop through the streets of Siena to the Cathedral, accompanied, according to a contemporary chronicler, by the sound of trumpets, clarionets and castanets.

The Adoration of the Magi

C. 1445

Fra Angelico and Fra Filippo Lippi

It is always intriguing to decipher a work which shows the hands of two major masters, and even more so when that painting exemplifies the revolution which took place in painting in Florence during the first half of the fifteenth century. Although much debate has surrounded its attribution, it is now agreed that work on the tondo commenced in the early 1440s, Fra Angelico (*c.* 1400–55) being responsible for the general composition. The figure of the Virgin and that of the infant Christ are undeniably from his hand: the sweetness of their expressions and delicacy of touch together with their small and fine features are clear trademarks of his style. In 1445 Fra Angelico was summoned to Rome by the Florentine Pope Nicholas V, and it seems likely that this panel was left unfinished on his departure to be completed by the youthful though radical Fra Filippo Lippi (*c.* 1406–69).

Apart from being a work of remarkable beauty, the painting contains elements both of the nascent early Renaissance style and the International Gothic tradition. The nude figures in the middle ground reflect the renewed interest in the human figure and Classical sculpture which prevailed in Florence at the time.

This picture is almost certainly the tondo cited in the Medici inventory of 1492 made on the death of Lorenzo the Magnificent, which is described as 'a tondo with its golden frame representing the Madonna and our Lord and the Magi offering gifts from the hand of Fra Giovanni (Angelico).' The painting was valued at one hundred florins, the highest price for any painting listed.

The Youthful David

C.1450

Andrea del Castagno

This remarkable work is painted on a leather ceremonial shield, which would have been used in processions prior to tournaments and other festive occasions. Although numerous painted shields exist from this period, this is the only one decorated by a great master. The dynamic figure of David shows Castagno (c. 1421/3–57) to have been at the forefront of Florentine painting in the mid fifteenth century.

The image of David is infused with symbolic meaning. Both the act of slaying and the dead giant are seen simultaneously in this image of the triumph of liberty over tyrannical force. The introduction of dynamic movement represents an important development in the history of painterly expression. David, shown on the point of letting fly his fatal stone, is one of the earliest action figures of the Renaissance, initiating a tradition embraced by artists of the subsequent generation, notably the Pollaiuolo brothers, Signorelli and ultimately, Michelangelo. It has been suggested that the pose of the figure owes much to the image of a horrified man from a Hellenistic sculptural group representing Niobe and her slaughtered children, which is now in the Uffizi. The play of the drapery around the body and the treatment of the hair are plausibly antique in inspiration. An unmistakable influence of a more contemporary kind is the sculpture of Donatello. The head of Goliath in particular is not dissimilar to that below the feet of Donatello's languid and elegant bronze *David* of 1440.

The Adoration of the Magi

c.1481

Sandro Botticelli

Painted nearly forty years after the tondo by Fra Angelico and Lippi (page 58), this Adoration scene is a product of the courtly elegance and intellectual refinement of the circle of Lorenzo de' Medici. It is one of five paintings of the theme by Botticelli (1444/5–1510) and is generally considered to be the finest. The work was probably painted while the artist was in Rome working on his frescoes in the Sistine Chapel for Pope Sixtus IV. Certainly some of the elements in the painting are very Roman. The architecture is reminiscent both of antique ruins and the great Roman basilicas such as old St. Peters. Similarly, the landscape background seems more evocative of the Roman Campagna than Botticelli's native Tuscany.

The lyrical line, such a hallmark of Botticelli's painting, is combined with a subtle compositional technique. The architectural perspective is exaggerated, leading the eye into the centre of the painting and the Holy Family, who are surrounded by the Magi and their entourage. It is worth observing that Botticelli has introduced a note of dynamic action in the writhing horses and their grooms on the right hand side of the composition, which counterbalances the serenity of the central part of the group.

This is a mid-career Botticelli, painted shortly after the famous mythological paintings *Primavera* and *The Birth of Venus*, before his work became mannered under the influence of religious fanatics in the 1490s. There are two fine portraits by the artist in the collection and a *Virgin and Child*.

This hauntingly beautiful portrait is one of the great treasures of the collection and, purchased in 1967, one of the newest masterpieces to adorn the walls of the National Gallery. It is the only painting by Leonardo outside Europe and is his earliest known portrait. As in so much of Leonardo's (1452–1519) work there is an air of magnificent mystery surrounding the painting. The sitter's identity is alluded to in the prominence given to the juniper bush seen behind her head and repeated in symbolic form on the reverse of the panel, since the name Ginevra is a dialect form in the feminine gender of *ginepro*, the Italian word for juniper. Vasari mentions a portrait of Ginevra in his life of Leonardo and there is no reason to doubt that this is the work to which he referred.

Equally cryptic is the mood of the sitter. Her white, mask–like face has an air of melancholy and even sadness about it, a mood rarely expressed in portraiture, particularly at this date. There is a plausible although somewhat romantic explanation for this. It was in March 1480 that Ginevra was deserted by her lover, the Venetian ambassador Bernardo Bembo; there is even a poem recounting their parting. Whether or not this is a valid interpretation, the mood is evident and accounts for the enigmatic spell cast by this image of withdrawn, refined and forever distant beauty. It is a work of which the gallery can be justifiably proud, a masterpiece from that most mercurial of painters with the most active and diverse mind recorded in European culture.

The Crucifixion

c.1481

Pietro Perugino

This beautiful triptych from the hand of the Umbrian Master was originally believed to be by his more celebrated pupil Raphael, whose youthful work closely resembled that of Perugino (*c.* 1445/50–1523). The painting, which was purchased from the Hermitage by Andrew Mellon, is known to have been given to the church of San Domenico in San Gimignano by one Bartolomeo Bartoli, who died when Raphael was only fourteen years old, thus confirming the attribution to Perugino. It is likely that the painting was executed in 1481 when Perugino was in Rome working on frescoes in the Sistine Chapel.

A hallmark of Perugino's style is the mood of tranquil veneration which pervades this devotional image. The figures of St. Jerome and the Magdalene occupy the side panels while those of the Virgin and St. John are either side of the crucified Christ. All are linked by a beautiful landscape which runs continuously through the three panels. The common use of pattern book figures in the Renaissance is exhibited here, the Magdalene assuming exactly the same pose as St. John.

The glory of the picture is the landscape, in which the influence of Flemish painting is evident. The outcrops of rock with elegant trees behind the subsidiary saints to the left and right give way to a wonderful vista of a river passing under a bridge and fortified town before flowing into the open sea.

THE NATIONAL GALLERY OF ART

This tondo is one of the supreme compositional achievements of Renaissance painting. It was painted when Raphael (1483–1520) was in Rome and very much under the spell of Michelangelo, who was working on the Sistine Chapel ceiling at the time. A famous anecdote from Vasari tells how the architect Bramante brought Raphael into the Chapel whilst the painting of the ceiling was in progress but Michelangelo, having argued with his patron Pope Julius II, had fled to Florence. The influence was made immediately manifest in Raphael's work and recognized as such by the jealous Michelangelo. Not only is the *Alba Madonna* close in composition and spirit to the Libyan and Erythraean Sibyls on the Sistine ceiling, but the compositional format could well owe something to Michelangelo's sculpted *Taddei Tondo* of 1504, now in the Royal Academy, London. The majesty of the figures, the clarity of line and the masterfully lucid spatial manipulation, confirm this painting as a mature Raphael of the first rank.

Raphael used a rhomboidal geometric format for the figure composition, which he set against an expansive landscape background. It is a dynamic shape which balances perfectly with the circular format of the painting as a whole. The equilibrium thus achieved is a fragile one, here perfectly realized. Raphael's work of this period has a flawless quality of formal perfection and mood which is without peer, and he will always be recognized as the quintessential High Renaissance painter.

The Feast of The Gods

1514

Giovanni Bellini and
Titian (Tiziano Vecellio)

Ovid describes how a group of Gods accompanied by nymphs and satyrs journeyed into the countryside in order to sacrifice an ass. On the right-hand side of the painting the god of fertility is attempting to lift the skirts of the goddess of chastity. His libidinous intentions, however, were frustrated by the braying of the ass and 'the nymph in terror started up ... and flying gave the alarm to the whole grove... the god in the moonlight was laughed at by all.' Sexual gestures and symbolism pervade the work, which has the warmth of colour and depth of tonality which are such marked characteristics of Venetian painting of the age of Giorgione.

The respective hands of the two Venetian masters are clearly identifiable. Titian (c. 1485–1576) clearly painted the background landscape and Bellini (c. 1430/40–1576) the foreground figures. The composition of the figures was conceived in the form of a Classical relief but this effect was altered by Titian, who also applied his hand to some of the figures. It is known that the work was painted for one of the alabaster rooms in the Castello in Ferrara and that the final payment for the painting was made in 1514. However, the style of the painting points to an earlier date and perhaps to a project conceived for the most famous woman of the Renaissance, Isabella d'Este, in 1509. Isabella subsequently commissioned Titian to execute a series of famous paintings with bacchanalian themes, and it seems probable that the alterations made by Titian, probably around 1530, were undertaken to blend in with the later works.

The Adoration of the Shepherds

c. 1505–1510

Giorgione (Giorgio Barbarelli)

Few artists as revolutionary as Giorgione (1476/8–1510) are as enigmatic. Nearly all the work which can be accurately ascribed to him has been lost, and few paintings are universally attributed to the master. The revolution effected by Giorgione was to create paintings of pure mood, usually for private contemplation and interpretation. His influence seems to have been immediate and profound, most notably in the work of Titian, who was to dominate Venetian painting for the best part of the sixteenth century.

For many years the attribution of this prized *Adoration* was the subject of dispute, and this was the source of a violent disagreement between the art dealer Lord Duveen and the great art historian Bernard Berenson. The latter was finally persuaded that the picture was largely the work of the mysterious Giorgione and it was bought by Samuel H. Kress, who donated it to the grateful gallery.

Giorgione has transported the nativity scene from the Holy Land to his native Veneto. The wonderful browns and greens of the landscape have a rich tonality which is offset by the tranquil devotional group in the centre. The figures and the cave seem to owe a great deal to Mantegna's *Adoration of the Magi* in the Uffizi in Florence, and the treatment of light to the late Giovanni Bellini. In the final analysis however, the picture is pure Giorgione in spirit and it is the meticulously painted warm landscape within which the devotional scene is set which is its crowning glory.

Venus with a Mirror

c. 1555

Titian (Tiziano Vecellio)

Titian's (1485–1576) long career is one of the greatest and most influential in the history of art. He initially trained in the workshops of the Bellini, and his vast oeuvre embraced the poetic moods and subtle tonality of Giorgione, absorbed the achievements of the Roman High Renaissance, and towards the end of his life achieved a mode of expression in the human figure which perhaps only Michelangelo among his contemporaries could rival.

Among the gallery's fine holding of the work of Titian is this mature nude executed when the artist was probably over seventy years old. Titian did not visit Rome until the mid 1540s, and this experience inspired a greater monumentality and classicism in his painting, which can be seen here. Titian was a man who understood and loved the feminine form, and the sensuality of this late image of Venus bears testimony to this. His mastery of the oil medium is exemplified in his handling of the ample flesh of the torso, shrouded with rich furs and velvets. This is a classical Venus, a Roman matriarch in the guise of the goddess of love, who in the privacy of her boudoir admires herself whilst being tended by adoring putti. She is the ideal of woman as conceived by a man of mature years, whose powers of painterly expression were undiminished by age.

Apollo Pursuing Daphne
c. 1765–66
Giovanni Battista Tiepolo

Although Venetian art never again attained the dizzy heights of its achievement in the sixteenth century, the Venetian painter Giovanni Battista Tiepolo (1696–1770) occupies an important place in the history of eighteenth-century painting. Tiepolo was the Rococo decorator *par excellence*, his style exhibiting a peerless elegance and bravura. Rich and animated, it exemplifies the spirit of eighteenth-century Venice which, having lost any political or economic significance, had become the European city of pleasure.

His daring style coupled with a dazzlingly clear palette established Tiepolo as the leading decorative painter of his age, executing work not only in and around his native Venice but also completing great fresco cycles in the Residenz at Würzburg and the Royal Palace in Madrid. In this picture, however, painted shortly after the completion of the Würzburg cycle, he was liberated from the restrictions of fresco technique, and working in the flexible medium of oil he was able to create a mythological scene of idealized sensuality. The delightful nude of the metamorphosing Daphne resting atop a Classical river God is being pursued by a radiant Apollo. The river god is her father who has arrived in time to rescue her. Cowering in the shadows to the left is Cupid, whose mischief has been the cause of the unfortunate event. The painting is a pendant to *Venus and Vulcan* in the Philadelphia Museum of Art, and there is a precise compositional relationship between the two.

The Needlewoman

c. 1640

Diego Velázquez

This delightfully intimate work presents a marked contrast to the large-scale court portraits and religious works one normally associates with the great Spanish painter. It is one of the few paintings Velázquez (1599–1660) executed for his own pleasure, and it betrays a remarkable and hugely appealing power of observation.

The sitter has been identified as the painter's daughter Francisca, who later married his pupil Juan Battista del Mazo, and the domestic nature of the portrait may well reflect the family relationship. The ruddy cheeks and softly illuminated breast are the focus of a wonderfully observed rendering of a young girl concentrating on her needlework. Although they appear unfinished the sketched out hands may well have been intentionally rendered in this way in order to convey rapid movement. The simple treatment also provides us with a valuable document of Velázquez's painting method. The large simplified zones of colour in the lower part of the painting create diagonals defining the space. The finely painted head, surmounted by a subtly placed red headband is bathed in a shimmering interior light. This painting may well be that listed as 'head of a woman sewing' in the inventory of Velázquez's effects at the time of this death.

The Gallery also possesses a *Portrait of Pope Innocent X*. It is interesting to compare this domestic portrait with the official image of the mighty pontiff, one of Velázquez's most famous subjects.

A Young Girl with her Duenna

c. 1655/60

Bartolomé Esteban Murillo

To a great extent the reputation of Murillo (1617/18–82) rests on religious or genre pictures imbued with a somewhat sickly sentimentality. These works were extremely popular in his own day and continued to be so until our present century. By way of contrast, this masterpiece of observation and spontaneous vision capturing a particular moment, is free from sentimentality, and shows what the artist was capable of when liberated from his popular formula.

Murillo uses the device of a frame within a frame to contain the subject of a beautiful, smiling young girl with her duenna, seemingly staring from an upstairs window at admirers in the street below. He has manipulated the light with great mastery as it falls squarely on the young girl's face and shoulders. One's eye is led through a strong diagonal from bottom right to top left. The girl's innocent and welcoming smile is contrasted with the animated expression of the duenna, revealed through eyes and cheek alone since her mouth is concealed behind her veil. It is a moment of pure human expression, captured by a painter of genius.

The painting was popularly known as *Las Gallegas*, the Gallicians, referring to the tradition that it represents two of the notorious courtesans in Seville who came from the Province of Galicia. Courtesans or no, the immense charm of the painting gives it a timeless, universal appeal.

The Annunciation

c. 1432–36

Jan van Eyck

The revolution effected in painting in Flanders in the early fifteenth century can to a great extent be attributed to the newly invented technique of oil painting. Jan van Eyck (d. 1441) was the greatest exponent of this new technique, and looking at this picture one is struck by the bewildering and painstaking detail with which everything is painted – the metallic texture of the archangel's embroidered garment, the delicacy of the hair, the light passing through the windows and the designs on the ceramic floor. The words of Gabriel and the Virgin Annunciate are embossed on the panel. Those of the latter are upside down so that they can be read by the descending dove. The colouring is almost beyond belief in its radiance, in particular the spectral colours of the angel's wings and the jewels which adorn his crown.

This *Annunciation* is, however, more than a display of technical mastery for it is imbued with a poignant and complex Christian message, manifest in symbol. The conception of the Son of God is seen as the point in history where the era of law gives way to the Christian era of grace; when the message of the Old Testament gives way to the New. To symbolize this, Van Eyck has painted the upper part of the church dark, illuminated by a single stained glass window with the image of God the Father. By contrast the lower section is brightly lit through three windows symbolic of the Trinity, in front of which descends the dove, symbol of the Holy Spirit.

Portrait of a Lady

c. 1455

Rogier van der Weyden

The clasped hands, the diaphanous veil falling in a delicate yet rigid line, the serpentine elegance of the eyelids and the small nose crowning full lips make this the finest portrait from Rogier's (1399/1400–64) hand. The head is set against a black background and the only concession to decorative detail is the scarlet girdle with a golden clasp the lady wears around her waist. The identity of the sitter is not known although it has been suggested that this is an image of Marie de Valengin, daughter of Philip the Good, Duke of Burgundy. Whether this is the case or not it would appear to have been painted by the artist shortly after his return from Italy, a visit which profoundly affected his art. Rogier was the most influential artist in Flanders in the generation following Van Eyck and this beguiling image is one of his masterpieces.

The Temptation of Saint Anthony

c.1555

Pieter Bruegel the Elder

The attribution of this work has often been contested as it does not fit comfortably into Bruegel's oeuvre and yet the quality of the brushwork and the subject tend to point to the hand of the master. The painting was probably executed in the early years of his career between 1555 and 1558. Although Bruegel (c. 1525–69) is most famous for his scenes of peasant life he also executed a number of works depicting diabolical and highly symbolic religious and moral subjects. In these he introduced strange and hybrid monsters similar to those of Hieronymus Bosch, a painter of the previous generation whose work is also represented in the Gallery. This influence is seen in the bizarre foreground figures, the flying monsters and wierd devils inflicting their onslaught on the chastized Saint.

Christ on the Cross

c. 1508–10

Mathis Grünewald

This painting, also known as *The Small Crucifixion*, is one of only about a dozen paintings by Grünewald (*c.* 1470/80–1528), an enigmatic but highly significant artist. The intensity of feeling in this small work has few parallels and its roots lie in the German Gothic tradition of religious expression. The bruised and emaciated body of Christ with his head bowed as he is suspended on the Cross from elongated arms, his nailed palms reaching up to the sky, is the embodiment of suffering for the sins of man. The contorted hands of the figure of St. John and the shrouded heads of the Virgin and Magdalene epitomize grief. The scene is set against a starlit but gloomy night sky. The painting was probably executed around 1510 when Grünewald was at work on his masterpiece, *The Isenheim Altarpiece*, now in Colmar.

Portrait of a Clergyman

1516

Albrecht Dürer

Dürer (1471–1528), whose work as an engraver and woodcutter was unsurpassed, had the ability not only to apply the precision of this training to every detail in his painting, but also to express a dimension beyond the mere appearance of the individual. Every hair is painted with loving care and Dürer here employs one of his favourite techniques, conveying the reflection of a window in the eyes of his sitter to show the light source and to animate the portrait.

A year after this picture was painted Martin Luther nailed his Ninety-five Theses to the door of Wittenburg Cathedral, sparking off the Protestant Reformation. It is tempting to see in the fixed gaze of the clergyman the theological turmoil which was to let itself loose on the continent of Europe with devastating consequences.

Daniel in the Lions Den

1615

Sir Peter Paul Rubens

Rubens (1577–1640) is the painter who best expresses the spirit of the Baroque age, and this work displays the finest elements of his style: an effortless brushstroke technique, masterful balance of colours and well-orchestrated composition. Despite the snarling of the lions and the prayers of Daniel, the scene is pure theatre. The bones are props and the cross-legged stance of the prophet reassures us that all this is merely a stage set rendition of the Bible story.

The painting is remarkably well documented. Rubens himself describes the picture in a letter written in 1618 as 'Daniel among many lions, taken from life. Original entirely by my hand.' The letter was addressed to Sir Dudley Carleton, the English Ambassador in the Hague, who was at the time forming an art collection for the future King Charles I. Carleton was in possession of a collection of antique sculptures and Rubens, who was most anxious to purchase them, ageed a price which included this painting. Shortly after Charles's accession, Carleton was made Viscount Dorchester, and by way of thanks gave the King this picture.

As a remarkable final chapter, the painting was purchased in the 1960s and brought to America. Unrecognized by its owner as being of value, the work was put up for auction. Before the sale took place an American dealer purchased the canvas directly from its owner for under one thousand pounds, so no export licence was required. The dealer enjoyed a fabulous profit on sale to the National Gallery of Art, where it is the pride of a fine Rubens collection.

Descent from the Cross

1653

Rembrandt van Rijn

The National Gallery's Rembrandt collection is very impressive, most of the paintings having been bequeathed by the Widener family. Rembrandt (1606–69) has been called the greatest illustrator of the Bible, and this painting is an outstanding example of the way in which he treated religious subjects. By 1653 his initial commercial success having declined, he had adopted a more intimate and expressive style of painting in which he was less concerned with pleasing his patrons than with experimenting with the psychological intensity. This work belongs to that late period and co-incidentally employs the same composition as a painting of the same subject executed twenty years earlier. In this painting Rembrandt enhances the dramatic effect by subtly altering his earlier composition, thereby creating a masterpiece of religious expression.

The nocturnal scene is illuminated by two areas of supernatural light. The bleached face of the swooning Virgin immersed in her bereavement to the right is balanced by light emanating from the body and shroud of Christ. Faces and activities are revealed in the half light rhythmically linking the two primary figures, and the Cross above. The inanimate and tortured body of Jesus is a foil for the expression of profound grief in the face of Nicodemus as he lowers the body of the dead Saviour. His red jacket in the centre of the composition provides the colour fulcrum for the composition and the shroud covering part of his forehead is a subtle natural touch. Rembrandt's use of a thick impasto on the crucified body is yet another expressive device.

The Girl with the Red Hat

1665–7

Jan Vermeer

This small and exquisite painting shows a mastery in the manipulation of light that is Vermeer's particular strength. Vermeer (1632–75) is a mysterious character about whom little is known. He is recorded as living and dying in Delft, is known to have been a Catholic and to have fathered eleven children. He painted few pictures, which were apparently mostly bought by a single collector whose name is now lost. He also dealt in pictures and died a bankrupt. Yet he is now regarded as the master of seventeenth-century Dutch genre painting.

Vermeer creates a shimmering, vitreous quality on his picture surface reminiscent of the ceramics which made Delft so famous. Out of a murky interior a pretty young girl with vibrant red hat and shimmering red lips stares out at us beguilingly. Vermeer has aimed the light source squarely on the side of the girl's face. There is a soft, almost indistinct quality in the outlines of the forms yet the artist is at the same time able to convey perfectly an impression of their substance and solidity. Vermeer's paint has been described as 'like condensations of light, dabs as fluid as quicksilver spilled from the tip of his brush'.

There is another painting in the National Gallery worthy of comparison. *The Young Girl with a Flute* is very similar to this picture, but may well have been executed by pupils.

Italian Comedians

C. 1720

Antoine Watteau

THE NATIONAL GALLERY OF ART

Occasionally in the history of Western art the birth of a new style has coincided with the emergence of an artist of genius who through an exploration of the new style has defined its form and future development. Such was the case with Antoine Watteau (1684–1721) and the emergence of the Rococo style in France. The lightness of touch in Watteau's art is one of its great qualities. In his finest work, the eye flutters over the delicate surface created through the subtlest rendition of reflected light. Watteau, who was born in Flanders, came to Paris at the age of eighteen and began work as a painter of theatrical scenes. From this experience he derived his interest in theatrical subjects and themes from the popular *Commedia dell'arte*, of which this is an example.

It has been suggested that this painting was executed for Watteau's personal physician, Dr Richard Meade, when the artist came to London in 1720 to consult him. He was by then certainly dying of tuberculosis, and this painting is full of pathos. In the centre of the composition is Pierrot, who looks at us and smiles without making the slightest gesture. Everything surrounding him is spinning around. The collection of faces and expressions is astonishing, each one as different and as fascinating as the other, set against an architectural background, a glimpse of landscape and a red curtain. Pierrot is at once the hero of the scene and at the same time the figure least concerned about it.

1735

Jean-Baptiste-Siméon Chardin

If Watteau represents the age of the Rococo through his depiction of a world of elegant fantasy, Chardin has his feet placed firmly on the ground. It is in his scenes of everyday life that we see another side of French life and art. Chardin (1699–1779) was the greatest of all French genre painters and a master of still life. There is a perfection in his work which, although it tends to depict the commonplace, holds our interest as if it were an elevated painting of an historical subject. He has been described as gilding with his brush the everyday life of the middle classes of eighteenth-century France.

In this painting Chardin has chosen the theme of concentration as the young boy with delicate features and elegantly dressed hair folds his cards to make an imaginary construction. The whole scene is very commonplace and yet has a Rococo vitality to it achieved through Chardin's clever play with light and space. Notice the careful illumination of the card table under the elbow of the boy and the open drawer which encroaches into our space, providing a link with the intimate scene beyond.

Chardin was championed by the writer and intellectual Diderot, who saw in his work a degree of moral refinement distinct from the mainstream court painting of the period, which appealed to his desire for an art with some social commitment and relevence. In this sense Chardin foreshadows the change in subject matter and in the general perception of the role of art which took place towards the end of the century.

A Young Girl Reading

c.1776

Jean-Honoré Fragonard

It is interesting to contrast this beautiful and intimate painting with a similar subject by Chardin (page 77), for although the art of Fragonard in many ways epitomizes all that is grand and sensuous in the French Rococo style, in this work he appears to have absorbed many of the qualities so admired in Chardin. This is evident in the quiet intimacy of the scene, the concentration of the girl, and the commonplace nature of her activity. The pose is simple and the figure, although elegantly dressed, wears no jewellery which might distract from the primary element of the subject. Where Fragonard (1732–1806) does differ markedly from Chardin, however, is in his dexterous brushwork and the flighty Rococo rhythms that this creates. The key to the rhythm is in the posture of the girl's fingers as she holds the book in her right hand, slightly awkwardly yet with an elegance which is repeated again in the folds of her sleeve and the bow in her hair.

This is one of a series of pictures representing girls in moments of solitude and relaxation which Fragonard painted in the 1770s when he was at the height of his power and popularity. The warm tonality of yellows, oranges and pinks, almost monocromatic in their range, are brilliantly manipulated to achieve a rich and luminous effect.

This famous portrait of Napoleon by David (1748–1825) was commissioned by the Scottish Duke of Hamilton at the height of the Napoleonic Wars. The commission was unorthodox, even treacherous, but the Duke had reason to hope that victory for Napoleon would mean a return to the Stuart line in England from which he was descended. He was also friends with the Emperor's sister Pauline.

Of the many portraits of Napoleon this is unique in its treatment. The Emperor aged about forty-seven is depicted in his study. The clock on the wall tells us that it is nearly quarter past four in the morning. One candle in the three-part candelabra has burned out and the other is burning low. 'You have understood me David' exclaimed Napoleon, 'By night I work for the welfare of my subjects, by day for their glory.' The detail in the picture is remarkable. The Emperor's uniform combines elements of the famous Imperial guard uniform with an infantry general's epaulettes; this was what he wore on special occasions and on Sundays. He sports the insignia of the Legion of Honour and the Iron Cross of Italy, two orders he created himself. Under the table is a copy of Plutarch's *Lives of the Great Republican Romans* and rolled up on the chair a copy of the *Code Napoleon*, the legal system he codified. In pre-Russian campaign France, it appeared that the ever-victorious general could bring nothing but glory. It is ironic that 1812, the year in which this portrait was painted, would bring the first dramatic reversals of his career.

Madame Moitessier

1851

Jean-Auguste-Dominique Ingres

Ingres (1780–1867) trained with David (see page 79) and then journeyed to Rome to complete his education. He was the great champion of the classical ideal in nineteenth-century French painting and his rivalry with the Romantic Delacroix provides one of the great stylistic juxtapositions in the history of art. Ingres was meticulous in the extreme and this is no better illustrated than by the four versions of the portrait of Madame Moitessier on which he worked for twelve years. He always strove for an elusive perfection.

Conceptions of beauty change over the years, and in mid nineteenth-century Paris Madame Moitessier was considered a woman of exceptional beauty. 'An artist's pencil was never entrusted with the task of reproducing features more beautiful, more splendid, more superb, more junoesque' wrote the poet Gautier. Ingres himself agreed and consented to paint her after some procrastination. He laboured for seven years on this portrait and even when it was completed in 1851 he immediately began painting another version, which now hangs in the National Gallery in London.

Ingres recreates Madame Moitessier as a Classical goddess removed from Mount Olympus to a Paris drawing room of the Second Empire. The glory of his style is in his wonderful understanding of line. The depiction of her rounded shoulders and the delineation of her plump arms and pearls against the black of her dress in the purest of statuesque poses is worthy of the formality of Raphael.

THE NATIONAL GALLERY OF ART

Many of the paintings we now most admire by Turner (1775–1851) were experiments in capturing meteorological and light effects and not meant for exhibition or public sale. This finished picture, however, represents another aspect of his art and was exhibited at the Royal Academy in 1827.

We are presented with a tranquil scene of the Thames on a summer evening. Barges are passing downstream towards London and the spectator is sitting in a garden bordered with a line of Claudean trees. As with so many of Turner's works it is the radiant sun which is the key to the painting, and the manner in which the light seemingly dissolves the solid matter of the wall is masterly.

There is an amusing anecdote relating to this painting. Close inspection reveals that the black dog and the parasol nearby are pieces of paper stuck on to the canvas. According to one story Landseer, the animal painter, placed the dog there when Turner was out of the room as a light-hearted jest prior to the opening of the Royal Academy exhibition. On his return Turner merely adjusted the animal, secured it to the canvas, and added some highlights to the black silhouette. What seems more likely, however, is that Turner noticed that he needed some form of visual punctuation mark in the centre of the work and affixed the dog to the canvas and went away. The paper possibly fell, only to be replaced by Landseer. It seems unlikely that a youngster like Landseer would have risked upsetting Turner, who was a venerable Royal Academician of some twenty-five years standing.

Brook Watson and the Shark

1778

John Singleton Copley

This remarkable painting is noteworthy for two reasons: first for its extra-ordinary subject matter and second for the fact that this was the work which established John Singleton Copley (1738–1815), a young artist from the American colonies, as a respected painter in the fertile environment of London in the 1770s. The painting met with great critical acclaim when it was exhibited at the Royal Academy in 1778.

Brook Watson, shown naked in the water, was only fourteen when in 1749 he was attacked by a shark in Havana Harbour. His right leg was severed below the knee and he narrowly avoided death, although according to contemporary reports he was totally recovered after three months. The painting shows him on the point of rescue. Having survived this encounter with the jaws of death, Watson went on to become a successful merchant in the colonies and in the City of London. He served both as Lord Mayor of London and as a director of the Bank of England, and he was made a baronet in 1803.

Copley, whose painting style made him a favourite with the City of London merchants, became a full member of the Royal Academy in 1781. He was one of the most popular and successful painters of his day, specializing in portraits and scenes of contemporary history. One of America's earliest great artists, Copley is well represented in the National Gallery.

The White Girl
(Symphony in White No.1)

1862

James Abbott McNeill
Whistler

Whistler (1834–1903) began painting this picture in Paris in 1861. He described the work to his friend George du Maurier early the following year: '... A woman in a beautiful Cambric dress standing against a window which filters the light through a transparent white muslin curtain – but the figure receives a strong light from the right and therefore the picture, barring the red hair, is one gorgeous mass of brilliant white.'

The painting caused a sensation when it was exhibited in Paris at the Salon des Refusés in 1863. The novelist Zola described how the public became almost hysterical with laughter in front it, although the critics were more enthusiastic. Fernand Desnoyers described it as 'a portrait of a spirit, someone who's psychic, the face, the bearing, the figure, the colour are strange. It is both simple and fantastic'. The painting is in fact a portrait of Whistler's mistress at the time, Joanna Hiffernan, and shows all the influences which were coming together to produce Whistler's own idiosyncratic style: Manet, the portrait tradition of Spain, Japanese prints and the Pre-Raphaelites, especially Dante Gabriel Rossetti. This marvellous work was the first of a series on the same theme showing beautiful girls in light infused interiors. The almost Japanese two-dimensionality and the contrast with the highly animated, though undoubtedly dead, wolf's head on the floor are striking.

The Biglin Brothers Racing

c.1873

Thomas Eakins

Of all the American painters working at the end of the nineteenth century, Eakins (1844–1916) was the most unashamedly academic and intellectual. As a student in Europe he was educated in the formal French salon style, but returning to the USA he came under different influences and became obsessed with anatomy of both humans and animals as well as photography. From 1871 to 1874 Eakins's concern with reflected light led him to study light refraction on water. This work belongs to this period and it is an integrated classical composition with a cohesive, geometrical balance of all its elements. It also provides us with a glimpse into life in late nineteenth-century Philadelphia, which is not without its charm.

Right and Left

1909

Winslow Homer

Always happiest painting subjects associated with the sea, Homer (1836–1910) created an individual style which appears to us to be typically American, unaffected by the academies of Europe, their champions and opponents. In 1883 he settled at Prout's Neck in the state of Maine, where he lived in isolation, quietly refining an art which will always be linked with the New England coastal landscape and with American natural scenery in general. In this work he has depicted two ducks shot in flight falling into the sea in a masterfully balanced composition whose harmony does not detract from the drama and urgency of the scene. This is American realism in its purest sense.

The National Gallery of Art contains a marvellous collection of paintings by the French Impressionists and their successors. Because of their visual accessibility and the charm of their subject matter, they are some of the most popular works in the collection.

Manet (1832–83) had outraged the Paris art establishment in the 1860s with his exhibits at the Salon des Refusés, so it was surprising when this painting was accepted for the official Salon exhibition of 1874. This direct scene of everyday life did, however, win more criticism than praise at that show. To the twentieth-century eye it is the freshness of treatment of the subject which is so arresting. The beautiful seated figure is Victorine Meurent, Manet's famous model who is familiar to us from the earlier paintings *Olympia* and *Déjeuner sur l'herbe*. She gazes at us directly, even quizzically, inviting us into the picture, her finger marking a page in the book, the puppy sleeping in her lap.

The little girl, the daughter of Manet's friend Adolphe Hirsch, is the key to the composition. The way in which she grasps at the railing indicates her absorption in the trains and the activity in the smoky station. It is an unseen yet masterfully conceived portrayal of the fascination that such things hold for a child. This is the first large canvas which Manet painted mostly out of doors, in accordance with Impressionist theory.

Bather Arranging her Hair

1893

Pierre-Auguste Renoir

Renoir (1841–1919) was one of the least consistent of the Impressionists. In some of his works painted in the 1870s he achieved a soft quality of light and human charm which is masterful and entirely original. Other paintings, particularly his portraits, have a wooden inanimate quality. The gallery boasts over thirty canvases from his hand including the famous *Girl with a Watering Can*, and a number of female nudes of which this explosion of colour and femininity is one of the finest examples.

In Renoir's late works the female nude became more and more his primary preoccupation and gave rise to some of his best paintings. He gave a fresh impetus to his painting of the subject, one of the most important themes in French art. By the time Renoir painted this wonderful canvas he had parted with the other Impressionists and their early theory and evolved a very personal style. This gloriously soft and sensuous female torso, bathed in the warm sunlight, is a celebration of the very essence of femininity. She is surrounded by discarded clothing in soft colours and the delicate green tones of the woods behind her provide a backdrop. Her head is lowered as she unties her hair. Renoir was working here with a favourite model with whom he was totally familiar and totally happy. He wrote that a painter benefits well from a model 'well worked into his brushes'.

THE NATIONAL GALLERY OF ART

In July 1888 Van Gogh (1853–90) wrote to his fellow artist Emile Bernard explaining that he had just finished this portrait: 'The girl is dressed in a jacket of blood red and violet stripes and a blue skirt with orange polka dots. In her hand is an oleander flower. I am so exhausted that I cannot even write.' He also wrote to his brother Theo about the painting: 'It took me a whole week, I have not been able to do anything else, not having been very well either.... but I had to reserve my mental energy to do the Mousmé well. A Mousmé is a Japanese girl, Provençal in this case, twelve to fourteen years old.'

Vincent had come down to Arles earlier in the year and was probably enjoying the happiest and most stable period of his life. He was obsessed with the lessons he had learned from Japanese prints and wrote to his brother about the clarity and simplicity he saw in them, which gave him inspiration to work with masses of flat tone. The painting has immense charm, and as well as deploying violent and expressive colouring the artist plays with the curving lines of the chair in which the girl is sitting. One disturbing element is the rather sickly withered quality of her hand grasping at the oleander, which is a fusion of yellow and green tones. The painting makes an interesting comparison with the *Entrance to the Public Gardens at Arles* (page 111), which was painted at the same time in the artist's life.

Fata Te Miti

1892

Paul Gauguin

It was an uncompromising quest for his own form of artistic expression which led Gauguin (1848–1903) to abandon his career as a stockbroker and devote his life fully to art. Leaving his wife and children, he set up an artistic community in Pont Aven in Brittany in 1886 in an attempt to find inspiration in the uncorrupted society of simple Breton peasants. Searching for an art free from convention and the trappings of European academic culture, he forsook Brittany for Martinique before travelling to the Polynesian island of Tahiti in 1891, where this canvas was painted.

Gauguin shows a group of Polynesians beside a vividly coloured sea. In the background is a fisherman while in the foreground one girl is diving into the sea whilst the other is removing her clothing. The colours are of a wondrous intensity not modulated at all, yet balancing harmoniously with one another, forming beautiful abstract patterns. Pinks, lilacs and purples in the foreground are contrasted with the splash of orange foliage and the brown bodies of the figures against the blue green of the breaking waves. The picture's title roughly translated means 'By the Sea'.

This painting was produced a few months after Gauguin's arrival in Tahiti. He had commenced a relationship with Tehura, a beautiful Polynesian girl, and it is suggested that she posed for the figure of the girl removing her sarong. Gauguin's period in Tahiti was a troubled one, plagued by illness and disillusionment. The South Seas did, however, inspire outstanding paintings such as this.

At seven foot square this is a very impressive painting, not only for its scale but also for its disturbing emotional content. It is one of the greatest achievements of the artist's youth. By 1905 Picasso (1881–1973) had abandoned his predominantly blue palette and replaced it with warmer tones, ushering in his so-called Rose period. Two years later he painted the violent and revolutionary *Demoiselles d'Avignon* (Museum of Modern Art, New York), the first Cubist painting.

Picasso had many friends in the Cirque Medrano and made many studies of them, using the characters in a number of his paintings. In this, the greatest of his works featuring the circus characters, he has placed the clowns, jugglers and strolling players in a desolate landscape, a featureless setting with no reference to space and time. The figures are alienated from one another with no compositional or emotional relationship, they either stare away or beyond one another. It is an objective vision. The use of circus characters is a pretext for the depiction of human situations 'wherein the external world is merely a mask laid over an underlying significance'. The unifying element of the composition is the seeming inner loneliness of the personages and their mood of detached contemplation. It has been suggested that the profile of Harlequin is a self-portrait.

Lavender Mist

1950

Jackson Pollock

In the late 1940s Jackson Pollock (1912–56) began producing paintings by dripping pigment onto a canvas laid flat on the floor. The resulting works, of which this is one of the finest examples, are some of the most original productions in American Art and the most recognizable of a style which became known as Abstract Expressionism. Pollock became the standard bearer of a new style of painting which for the first time established New York as the centre of contemporary Western art. His technique in creating his works was to swing the paint stick or some other tool so that the paint splattered onto the canvas. 'On the floor', he declared, 'I am more at ease, I feel nearer, more a part of the painting, since this way I can walk around it, work from the four sides and literally be in the painting.' Pollock called his technique 'automatic response' and further elaborated 'When I am in my painting, I am not aware of what I am doing. It is only after a sort of "get acquainted" period, that I see what I have been about. I have no fears about making changes, destroying the image because the painting has a life of its own'. It is apparent that the painting's 'life of its own' was very much the product of the artist's conscious idea and technique. It is this control which created the complex patterns on the surface of the canvas which in paintings such as this are of great beauty and delicacy.

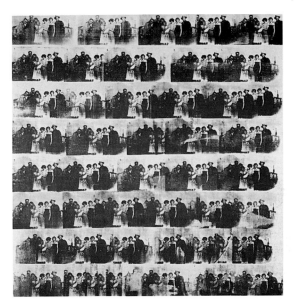

Warhol (1928?–87) is the best known artist of Pop culture, a culture of disposable images, product packaging and the triviality of media fame. He challenged our perception of art by throwing these seemingly banal symbols of twentieth-century life in the face of the art world. The Gallery contains two of Warhol's most famous icons, the *Campbell's Soup Cans* and the celebrated *Marilyn*, both produced in 1962.

Early in the 1960s Warhol developed a style of silkscreening photographic reproductions onto canvas. These were repeated again and again to form a continuous frieze of images overlain one on top of the other. He used this technique in numerous works depicting accidents and incidents of horror and also in the electric chair series of the same date. The significance of these was that they forced people to re-examine the kind of photographs seen in newspapers or other reproduced disposable images. In New York Warhol came into contact with the Texan Pop artist, Robert Rauschenberg, who became his friend and mentor. He produced several series of works around the theme of his fellow artist, in this case derived from an old photograph of Rauschenberg's family. The photographs vary in texture and fuse into one another like flickering images on a black-and-white TV screen, underlining how they can be duplicated infinitely. This is the essence of Warhol's kind of Pop and his view of how the consumerist world of the later twentieth century should be reflected in art.

Address
950, Independence Ave SW,
Washington D.C.
 (202) 357 2700

Map reference
⑳

How to get there
Metro: Smithsonian

Opening times
Daily 10–5.30. Closed
Christmas Day

Entrance fee
Free entrance

Tours
Daily tours. Enquire at the
information desk

Opposite the Sackler Gallery on the Smithsonian quadrangle is the domed National Museum of African Art. The Museum was started as a private institution by Warren M. Robbins in 1964, first exhibiting in the former home of black abolitionist Frederick Douglas on Capitol Hill. In 1979 it became part of the Smithsonian, moving to the current site in 1987. The collection contains 6000 objects as well as the Elliot Eliosfen archives of 300,000 images of African art and culture. There is a rotating exhibition of the permanent collection on the first level, and the galleries on the second level are used to mount temporary exhibitions. The major stress of the museum is on the traditional arts of Africa south of the Sahara, including Zaire, Mali, Angola, Ghana and the Ivory Coast. The art of North Africa is also represented as are the ancient and contemporary arts of the entire continent. The display of objects is mounted thematically, and deals with such topics as spiritual beings and divination, masks and mask performances, rites of passage and personal adornment.

African art is totally different in approach from the Occidental or Oriental traditions and the museum attempts to emphasize this. Most of the objects created in sub-Saharan African culture are imbued with some kind of religious significance and perform a ritual function. Artworks are used to link the realms of the living with those of the dead and perform a role in ensuring the afterlife. Many African cultures use such objects as sculpted images to preserve values and beliefs from generation to generation, and these objects are generally infused with symbolic meanings. The museum's emphasis is less on individual pieces than an attempt to illustrate a complex culture through the exhibits which are not only decorative but which often radiate immense energy and power.

This impressive mask made of wood, fibre and metal is a ritual object and part of a larger costume which would probably have been worn by one performer in a dance. Masked dancers are often seen as the incarnation of ancestor or nature spirits. They are involved in such ceremonies as initiations and burials and they also oversee legal cases. In west and central Africa from where this mask originates such costumes are used to call up supernatural beings and consequently the wearer becomes possessed by the mask's spirit. Rites and rituals that use masks may celebrate important transitions in life such as the birth of a child, entrance into adulthood, or death. They can also be used to invoke human fertility or a fine harvest.

Aesthetically the mask in question is a particularly fine example, with sensitively carved features, large white circles around the horizontal slits for eyes, a thin delicate nose and a profusion of matted hair behind. This is one of numerous masks of different kinds in the collection. To Western eyes the mask is probably the object most immediately associated with African culture and such objects as this exerted a great influence on the painters of the early twentieth century. Picasso, Matisse and Modigliani in particular recognized the visual power of such masks, and used their forms in paintings and sculptures.

Address
8th St and G St. NW.
Washington D.C.
✆ (202) 357 2700.

Map reference
㉑

How to get there
Metro: Gallery Place

Opening times
Daily 10–5.30. Closed
Christmas Day

Entrance fee
Free entrance

Tours
Guided tours available Mon
to Fri at 12 and Sat and Sun
at 2

This museum has had a rather checkered history, but today it is one of the most enjoyable collections in Washington. In 1836 John Varden, a Washingtonian who wanted to improve the cultural climate of the fledgling capital, set up a gallery in his own home, calling it the Washington Museum. Six years later this was incorporated into the National Institution, a strange amalgam of *objets d'art* and natural history specimens which became part of the Smithsonian in 1858 and was housed in the recently built Castle on the Mall. The art holdings of the Smithsonian became the National Gallery of Art in 1906, and after several vicissitudes and changes of name, in 1968 this nomadic collection was finally named the National Museum of American Art and rehoused in the grand Doric building which was the Old Patent Office, a building it appropriately shares with the National Portrait Gallery.

The holdings are vast, comprising over 34,000 works by American artists ranging from the bizarre creations of outsider art to traditional images of American culture such as paintings by Frederic Remington and the Hudson River School. There is a good collection of primitive and colonial paintings, nineteenth-century masters including Whistler, Sargent, Winslow Homer and the American Impressionists. The paintings of the American West, which were so popular in the nineteenth century and which did so much to create the myth of that land, are well represented, including the mighty panoramic landscapes of Thomas Moran and Albert Bierstadt. The upper floor contains an outstanding display of twentieth-century American art and most of the major figures from the beginning of the century to the present day are shown.

In 1830 George Catlin (1796–1872) abandoned his legal career to explore the lands west of the Mississippi with the primary aim of recording the customs and way of life of native Americans. Over the next six years he acquainted himself with nearly all the native tribes of that vast region, gathering together a collection of paintings and drawings recording all aspects of Red Indian life and customs. This he complemented with a written narrative and an extensive collection of ethnographic objects.

This oil of Comanche warriors is a good example of his work. 'The Comanche' he wrote, 'is able to drop his body upon the side of his horse at the instant of passing his enemy, effectively screened from their weapons, as he lays in a horizontal position behind the body of his horse, with his heel hanging over the horse's back, by which he has the power of throwing himself up again and changing to the other side if necessary.' Catlin continues: 'I am ready without hesitation to pronounce the Comanches the most extraordinary horsemen that I have seen and I doubt very much whether any people in the world can surpass them.'

Catlin's pessimistic vision of the fate of native Americans was cruelly prophetic. He travelled with his Indian gallery throughout the major cities of the eastern United States and then went to Europe, championing the cause of a people he had grown to love and respect. He died aged seventy-seven, unrecognized and persecuted for his sympathetic attitude towards the native Americans.

Le Trajet

1911

Romaine Brooks

Romaine Brooks (1874–1970) was ignored for many years, but awareness of her art was rekindled by a gift to the National Museum of American Art by Laura Dreyfus Barney in the 1960s. This led to an exhibition of her work and a bequest from the artist herself. As uncompromising in her art as in her unorthodox sexuality, her best work like *Le Trajet* (translated as 'The Crossing') possesses a unique and intense, though perhaps melancholic, beauty.

After an unhappy childhood and sham marriage, Romaine Brooks became a part of the Paris intellectual set just prior to World War One, where she fraternized with the likes of Jean Cocteau and Gabriele D'Annunzio. One of that number, the Duc de Montesquieu, dubbed her 'the thief of souls'. In 1909 Diaghilev brought his *Ballets Russes* to Paris, with the beautiful Ida Rubinstein as part of the Company. Romaine found in her the 'living incarnation of her aesthetic ideal' and it is highly likely that it is her elegant though sickly body which is depicted in *Le Trajet*. This is the artist's homage to death, the ultimate journey celebrated in an almost dreamlike setting composed of black, white and grey. The painting has a linear design reminiscent of Art Nouveau, especially where the hair falls over the edge of the wing-like bed where the figure is lying. As in much of Romaine Brook's art, here we are confronted with a detached apprehension of beauty poisoned by tragedy, illness and death.

Few museums in the world have been founded in such a spirit of self-conscious idealism. Unashamedly feminist, the Museum has a mission to 'bring recognition to the achievements of women artists of all periods and nationalities by exhibiting, collecting, preserving and researching art by women and by educating the public as to their achievements.' It cannot be disputed that by its very existence the museum challenges the unequal representation of female artists in other museums and galleries. Moreover, the irony that the seven storey Beaux-Arts building was once the masonic temple of Washington is not lost on the organizers.

The Museum was founded by Wallace and Wilhelmina Holladay and opened in 1987. The guiding principle was elucidated by Wilhelmina who described it as 'the first museum in the world dedicated to the contribution of women to the cultural life of their society.' With this in mind it is not surprising that the permanent collection is largely revisionist, 'determined to give more than lip service to the happy phenomenon that for five thousand years art and creativity have been the province of both sexes.' Commencing on the third floor the collection is arranged in chronological order. Great efforts have been made to collect paintings by women artists working in the sixteenth and eighteenth centuries, and examples by painters of the first rank such as Lavinia Fontana, Rosalba Carriera and Elisabeth Vigée-Lebrun are on display. The nineteenth-century collection has paintings by great artists such as Mary Cassatt and Berthe Morisot. Naturally the largest section is devoted to the twentieth century with works by Helen Frankenthaler, Frida Kahlo, Bridget Riley and many others. The mezzanine has exhibition space for sculpture and silverware and the decorative arts, and there are further galleries for temporary exhibitions.

Address
1250, New York Avenue, Washington D.C.
✆ (202) 783 5000

Map reference

How to get there
Metro: Metro Centre

Opening times
Mon to Sat 10–5; Sun 12–5. Closed Thanksgiving, Christmas and New Years Day

Entrance fee
Suggested donation: adults $3, children and seniors $2

Tours
Two are given daily by reservation only

Dissertation in Insect Generations and Metamorphosis in Surinam

1719

Maria Sibella Merian

There were few opportunities for female artists prior to the twentieth century, but some remarkable women pursued careers in this field and a good number of their works are represented in the museum. Maria Sibella Merian (1647–1717) is doubly extraordinary, for she is as important in the history of the natural sciences as in the history of art, both of which were virtually the exclusive domain of men in the seventeenth and eighteenth centuries.

Maria Sibella Merian was born in 1647, the daughter of a topographical engraver and publisher. On the death of her father, her mother remarried a Dutch painter and the family moved to Nuremberg. Maria, who was twenty-three by this time, had started making oil and watercolour paintings of flowers, fish and insects. She was pursuing a dual career of flower painting and scientific research into the life cycles of insects. At that time it was popularly believed that insects generated themselves spontaneously from dirt or mud, a supposition confounded by Sibella's observations. She published her research in three illustrated volumes from 1679 to 1717. The illustrations she produced were revolutionary in that on a single page she showed each creature in all stages of metamorphosis on or near its preferred plant. This was to become the model for subsequent zoological and botanical illustrations.

In 1690 she moved to Amsterdam where she became a luminary of the city's artistic and scientific community. Under the auspices of that city she embarked on a two-year scientific voyage to Surinam in 1699, publishing her findings in a 1705 volume entitled *The Metamorphosis of Insects in Surinam*, from which this folio comes.

Mother Louise Nursing her Child

1899

Mary Cassatt

This delightful print displays well Mary Cassatt's mastery at capturing the intimate domestic scene with utmost delicacy. Few artists have been able to convey the unique relationship between mother and child with the same understanding and charm as Mary Cassatt (1844–1926), for whom it was a favourite theme. One of the finest female artists of the nineteenth century, she came from a well-to-do Pittsburgh banking family. After initial training in Pennsylvania, she undertook a tour of Europe, and in 1874 settled in Paris to study painting. She became friends with some of the leading figures of the Impressionist movement, with whom she exhibited. Degas in particular was a great influence on her and also a great admirer. This drypoint, with its delicate rendering of line and tone, illustrates some of the finest qualities in her art.

Portrait of a Girl in a Hat

1920

Marie Laurencin

Through her association with the poet and critic Guillaume Apollinaire, Marie Laurencin (1885–1956) became intimately bound up with the Cubists, particularly Picasso, in the early years of this century. Her affair with Apollinaire ended in 1913 and she fled France, only returning in 1920. Over the next seventeen years her artistic production reached its height. This delightful painting, often described as a self-portrait, comes from this period. It is very typical of the rather decorative style which she developed in the 1920s. The profile of the girl with a sweet snub nose and delicate pink lower lip is delicately drawn as a two-dimensional pattern against a mottled grey background. As well as being a painter Laurencin was also a prolific book illustrator and worked in the theatre, designing stage sets and costumes for Diaghilev's *Ballets Russes*.

Self Portrait

c.1921

Käthe Kollwitz

This brooding self-portrait is an excellent example of Kollwitz's (1867–1945) highly expressive etching style. She had a lifelong interest in the self-portrait in which her psychological insight has parallels in Goya and Rembrandt. In the late 1890s she came under the influence of Max Klinger, finding inspiration in his preoccupation with the trials of life. She endorsed his view that the darker side of life was best illustrated through the use of the graphic arts and gave up painting to devote the rest of her artistic life to printmaking and sculpture. Her themes are those of suffering, social injustice and war. A convinced pacifist, she suffered the tragedy of a son killed in World War One and a grandson in World War Two. Appropriately, her most famous sculpture is the bronze war memorial at Essen in Flanders.

Alligator Pears in a basket .

1923

Georgia O'Keeffe

Georgia O'Keeffe (1887–1986) was born near Sun Prairie in Wisconsin. In 1917 her art was noticed by the influential New York dealer, Alfred Stieglitz, who gave her a first exhibition. They were married in 1924. This bold charcoal drawing belongs to this early period. Clear in its forms and rich in tonality, it is an example of her ability to depict objects from the natural world in a fresh and original way. Later in her career she used the desert landscape and the elements found therein in her work, and a good example is the *Goats Horn with Red* (page 6) Equally famous are her enormously enlarged and highly sensuous colour studies of flowers, looking like vast abstracted landscapes or organic shapes, taken from hugely magnified natural objects.

The imposing Doric structure of the Old Patent Office building of Washington is now the home of the National Portrait Gallery, a building it shares with the National Museum of American Art (page 94). This is a singularly appropriate pairing as the portraits are largely the work of American painters, photographers and illustrators and number amongst them some outstanding pictures in their own right. Notable in this respect is the *Self-portrait* by John Singleton Copley and the wonderful portrait of the artist Mary Cassatt by Edgar Degas. The real aim of the Gallery, however, is to chronicle American history and culture through its leading citizens.

A visit should begin on the second floor with the presidential portraits, since the presidents naturally occupy a special position in American history and the celebrated Washington portraits hold pride of place. The exhibition follows a chronological sequence through American history, presenting rooms with themes such as fine arts and literature, the founding fathers, colonial America, politicians and explorers of the nineteenth century, the inventors and business barons of the gilded age, political and social reformers.

Up on the third floor is the Great Hall decorated in high Victorian style with ceramics and panels depicting sources of man's technology, as this room was originally designed to exhibit small models of patented inventions. On the mezzanine floor above is a section of the museum devoted to portraits associated with the Civil War period. From this comes the famous image of Abraham Lincoln (page 103). Back on the first (or ground) floor, great figures from the twentieth-century world of sports and the performing arts are featured in paintings, drawings, photographs and cartoons. The Gallery also mounts temporary exhibitions and these occupy the vaulted space on this floor

Address
F St and 8th St
NW, Washington D.C.
 (202) 357 2700

Map reference
(23)

How to get there
Metro: Gallery Place

Opening times
Daily 10–5.30. Closed
Christmas Day

Entrance fee
Free entrance

Tours
Guided tours every
45 minutes Mon to Fri
10–2.30 by request. Sat and
Sun at 11.15

George Washington

1796

Gilbert Stuart

This is without doubt the most celebrated of all presidential portraits. It is also generally believed that this unfinished version is the best likeness of the soldier and gentleman farmer turned statesman. This portrait with its companion, Martha Washington, was painted from life on April 12 1796. It was ostensibly a study for the full length 'Landsdowne Portrait' of Washington which also hangs in the National Portrait Gallery. The likeness is the basis for the image of Washington on the one dollar bill.

Gilbert Stuart (1755–1828) was born in America but trained as a portrait painter under his compatriot Benjamin West in London. He achieved a fine reputation, particularly due to the success of a portrait entitled *The Skater* painted in 1782 and the sensation of the Royal Academy exhibition of that year, now in the National Gallery of Art. His great profligacy drove him seriously into debt and he was forced first to leave England for Ireland, returning to America in 1793. 'I hope to make a fortune by Washington alone' Stuart informed his worried creditors. Indeed he did, for the portrait of Washington became a symbol of patriotism and there is an example in virtually every major gallery in the United States. The portrait replicas became known as 'Stuart's hundred dollar bills' as that was the price he charged for them.

This painting is shared with the Museum of Fine Arts in Boston. The exhibition of the work is rotated every three years and when the picture is in Boston it is replaced by Stuart's famous portrait of Thomas Jefferson.

Abraham Lincoln

1865

Alexander Gardner

Four days after this famous photograph was taken, Abraham Lincoln was shot whilst attending a performance at Ford's Theatre, and it is generally believed to be the last known portrait of him. Alexander Gardner (1821–82) was a local Washington photographer and this is a particularly telling portrait of the sixteenth President of the United States, who stares out with his characteristic goatee beard, heavily lined face, and deep set though rather weary eyes. The Gallery has many famous photographs in its collection, but perhaps no other has such significance for ordinary Americans than this image of a tired man who was shortly to lose his life for the preservation of the Union and the emancipation of the slaves. This albumen silverplate is the only print made from the negative, which cracked whilst the print was being processed.

John Pierpoint Morgan

1903

Edward Steichen

America is the land of great corporations, and no figure in the history of the USA exemplifies big business to a greater degree than John Pierpont Morgan, the venerable financier gauntly portrayed here. Morgan was the master of the merger, who founded one of the most famous and largest banking groups in the world, and was the prime mover behind the creation in 1901 of U.S. Steel, then the world's largest corporation. Morgan intially rejected Steichen's (1879–1973) photograph because of his fierce expression and what appears to be a knife reflecting in the arm of the chair. However, when Alfred Steiglitz published the image it received geat critical acclaim. Morgan recanted his previous view and offered to buy a print for $5000. Steichen refused. The photograph became one of the most admired of all his works.

Self Portrait

1903

Edward Hopper

Like Winslow Homer of a previous generation, Hopper (1882–1967) is an artist who is unmistakeably American, and he created a highly original and very influential style during a career spanning six decades. Hopper's art is often categorized as realism, but even though his subject matter is unspectacular and comes from an experience of everyday life, there is an intense psychological element which pervades all his work even when there are no figures painted on the canvas. His art also has a lonely desolate quality about it as it focuses on faceless cities, the run-down late night bar or diner, solitary figures in empty hotel rooms, or in a masterpiece like *Cape Cod Evening* (page 9) a brooding intensity of mood that goes beyond time and place. His people are more types than individuals and his places equally unspecific. Hopper once said that his aim in painting was 'the most exact transcription possible of my most intimate impressions of nature.'

This self-portrait was done in 1903 whilst he was a student at the New York School of Art studying under Robert Henri. The powerful charcoal drawing in three-quarter profile, one side of his face immersed in shadow, is one of a number of self-portraits which the artist made during his career.

The Octagon is one of Washington's oldest and finest Federal style residences. It was commissioned for a wealthy citizen, John Tayhoe, who had been persuaded by his friend George Washington to purchase one of the plots in the new city. Built between 1799 and 1801 it was designed by Dr William Thornton, the first architect of the Capitol, and became Tayhoe's winter residence. The Octagon is something of a misnomer in that the building is in fact six-sided with an elegant rounded front pavilion and it is appropriate that the former residence should now house the headquarters of the American Institute of Architects; they now use it both as administrative offices and as a series of exhibition rooms mostly for temporary displays. The circular study on the second floor is known as the Treaty of Ghent Room as President James Madison is supposed to have signed the peace treaty which ended the war between the British and Americans in 1815 on the round mahogany table in the centre of the room.

Address
1799 New York Avenue. NW,
Washington D.C.
 (202) 638 3105

Map reference
㉔

How to get there
Metro: Farragut West,
Farragut North

Opening times
Tue to Fri 10–4. Sat and
Sun 12–4. Closed on Mon
and major holidays

Entrance fee
Suggested donation: adults
$2; students and seniors
$1; children under 12 $0.50

Address
1600 21st St NW,
Washington D.C.
✆ (202) 387 2151 Visitor
info (202) 237 0961

Map reference

How to get there
Metro: Dupont Circle

Opening times
Tue to Sat 10–5. Sun 12–7.
Closed Mon, Thanksgiving,
Christmas, New Years Day
and 4 July

Entrance fee
Suggested Contribution:
adults $6.50, students and
seniors $3.25. Children
under 18 free

Tours
Guided tours Wed and
Sat at 2

Of all the great collectors who are mentioned in this book, Duncan Phillips stands out as the one with the greatest understanding of the art he and his wife collected. His informed and lucid comments which accompany the paintings perform the double function of describing both the work of art and the vision of its owner. It is the personal nature of the collection which is one of the great joys of the gallery, which still feels like a family home even though it has been used exclusively as a museum since 1930.

Duncan Phillips, who like Andrew Mellon came from Pittsburgh, was the grandson of James Laughlin, co-founder of the Jones and Laughlin Steel Company on which the family's wealth was based. In 1896 the family moved to Washington and took up residence in the much altered building which houses the collection. In 1916 Duncan and his brother James persuaded their parents to devote a small proportion of their income to collecting works of art under their guidance. The following year their father died, and in 1918 James lost his life. Deeply shocked by this dual bereavement, Duncan conceived the idea of the Phillips Memorial Gallery, which he opened to the public in 1921. Phillips and his painter wife Margaret collected avidly and passionately right up until Duncan's death in 1966. The stress of the collection is twentieth-century and there was a concerted policy to purchase the work of American as well as European masters. It is, however, the Impressionist and Post-Impressionist paintings which are the most famous, and one should not overlook the works by Old Masters such as El Greco, Chardin and Ingres, which are on display.

Although his enthusiasm was for late nineteenth- and early twentieth-century painting, Duncan Phillips was particularly fond of this canvas. He used to say that he could 'almost hear Constable's shout of exuberance as he was painting it.' To Phillips, he was the best of all British artists, 'the acknowledged discoverer of naturalistic landscape and the first to sense the freshness and immediate impact of nature.' In the early years of the nineteenth century such a work as this with its free brush technique would have been a sketch certainly not meant for sale or exhibition. Constable (1776–1837) was the quintessential painter of the English countryside, and despite the fact that he was lauded in France to a far greater extent than in contemporary England, he never left home shores. This kind of painting well illustrates Constable's own words: 'The sound of water escaping from Mill dams, old rotten banks, shiny posts and brickwork – these scenes made me a painter, and I am grateful.' All those elements can be seen in this painting of Constable's familiar landscape on the Stour between East Bergholt and Dedham in Suffolk. The worship of nature which was so much a part of the Romantic movement in Europe found particular expression in the work of the English landscape masters such as Constable, and was also an important influence on the Impressionists.

The Uprising

c. 1850–55

Honoré Daumier

This was one of Duncan Phillips's favourite paintings. It is a very large canvas for Daumier (1808–79) and its overtly political content recalls the heady revolutionary days of 1848. It expresses the strength of good men made desperate; these are the masses in revolt. Phillips spoke about the painting during the dark days of 1940 at a symposium entitled 'The place of the arts in the world today'. For him *The Uprising* 'depicts the volcanic explosion of all enslaved people everywhere. The Paris of its background might be the tragic Europe of today.... The magnetic agitator of its focus is the rallying point for the uprisings of tomorrow, pent up now and ready to burst.' He continues 'The leader of Daumier's picture is the eternal nomad of the questing spirit. Blind to the immediate perils of his position, haunted by his dreams of the future, he is the anonymous standard bearer of innumerable battles without name. He is pure flame, such fire will liberate and cleanse the world.'

Daumier was arguably the greatest caricaturist in Western art. His numerous lithographs cover the whole range of satire from his famous image of King Louis Philippe as a pear to the humorous jabs at bourgeois life he produced when censorship deprived him of political expression. In his oils, however, he adds an extra dimension to his art. As Balzac once wrote of him, 'He is a man who has something of Michelangelo in his blood'. It is the ability to seize a universal human message in a specific image which is his great talent and which he displays in this painting.

Although he exhibited with the Impressionists, Degas (1834–1917) belongs firmly to the classical tradition. This was not least because he was a pupil of that doyen of classicism in nineteenth-century France, Ingres. As his style developed so he concentrated on a variety of subjects, breaking free from history painting in order to concentrate on more contemporary themes like his friend Manet. Amongst these were ballet dancers, the races, the toil of working people and female nudes in a domestic setting. This work belongs to the intimate portraits which also form an important part of his oeuvre. Here he has captured a meditative, introspective state of mind: an expression of troubled sadness as indicated by the title. The figure clasps at her body pressed tightly against a chair. She slumps forward, a glow from the light source probably emanating from a fireplace warmly illuminating the russet colour of the furniture and her dress. A comparison with *The Ballet School* in the Corcoran Gallery (page 23) is interesting for the latter is much more representative of Degas's work as a whole.

Degas, who had an independent income, was free from the commercial restraints of his fellow Impressionists. Nor indeed did he ever fully embrace the tenets of Impressionism. He merely adopted aspects of their painterly practice to his own style. The emotional intensity of this painting, although highly effective and moving, was rare for Degas. It is worth noting that the title is not Degas's own but given to the work at a later date.

⭐ The Luncheon of the Boating Party

1881

Pierre-Auguste Renoir

This painting is the most famous in the collection and is indeed a work with such popular appeal that it is universally known and loved. Perhaps more than any other image of Impressionist era, the work expresses the comfort and pleasure of bourgeois life on a balmy summer afternoon on the Seine, accompanied by fine wine and good company. It is little surprise that Renoir's son Jean decided to animate such a painted scene fifty years later in his film *La Partie de Campagne* and imbue it with the same atmosphere.

By the time he painted it, Renoir (1841–1919) had broken free from the ideals of Impressionism which had coloured his earlier work. His concern here is for detail and in subtly observed human interrelationships. To some degree unity is lost for the sake of incident, but there are some wonderful passages: the glimpse of the river under the flapping awning, the pretty girl talking to her terrier and the dreamy, loving gaze of the girl leaning on the railing. Her eyes focus on the bowler-hatted gentleman whose head forms the fulcrum of the composition.

The painting was from the beginning one of Duncan Phillips's favourite works and in many ways the central axis about which the collection developed. His wife remembers an incident when Lord Duveen wanted to buy the picture and present it to the National Gallery in London. With typical Duveen flamboyance he waved a blank cheque in front of Phillips, saying 'fill in any amount you want.' She concludes, 'Naturally with our great feeling for the painting there was no chance for Duveen'.

In the summer of 1888 Van Gogh (1853–90) moved to Arles in the Provence region of France, and this is generally regarded as one of the happiest periods in his otherwise tormented and disturbed life. His art was developing in a manner which pleased him as well, with a new control of line and especially colour, as the warm vibrant colours of the Mediterranean landscape gave him fresh inspiration. It was in this period that he painted this small, wonderfully expressive scene. Van Gogh was very productive during these months. Possibly referring to this painting, he wrote to his brother Theo: 'The last picture done with the last tubes of paint on the last canvas, of a garden, green of course, is painted without pure green, nothing but Prussian blue and chrome yellow.'

Duncan Phillips was particularly fond of this work, and wrote of it: 'How to catch that pulse of nature, the repetition, the wave like ripples of the heat, the saturated glaze of the soil along the garden walk, the pungent, aromatic fragrance, the scintillant opulent colours, blues and greens, yellows and oranges in full cry under the sun, the trees of many shapes and textures, at the depths of which one could plunge and find shelter in the inner recesses of a cool shadow. How blue black the men and women look in the hot light, silhouetted in grotesque colours like the peasants of Hokusai against sunlit spaces.'

Deer in a Forest 1

1913

Franz Marc

Franz Marc (1880–1916) was a member of the *Blaue Reiter* (Blue Rider) Expressionist group, which he founded with Kandinsky in Munich in 1911. He was able to absorb the world of innocent animals into the context of a twentieth-century art movement and aimed to combine the forces of God and Nature within the framework of his own visual language. The forest has been transformed into an abstracted articulation of colour and form. The light as it passes through the trees becomes a myriad spectral pattern of greens, reds, yellows and blues. This is an almost pantheistic vision, with the tranquil elegance of the deer and a beautiful bird gliding overhead. It is perhaps ironic to detect a strong air of pacifism and innocence in Marc's work, for in 1916, at the age of only thirty-six, he was killed in action at Verdun.

The Open Window

1921

Pierre Bonnard

Pierre Bonnard (1867–1947) was one of Duncan Phillips's favourite artists and the collection of his paintings is an outstanding feature of the gallery. His wonderful colour sense found full expression in the balmy environment of the south of France, where he lived and worked for most of his life. He applied his style to aspects of his domestic life, nearly always featuring his wife, in intimate interiors bathed in the light of the Mediterranean. Here we are in a richly coloured room, his sleeping wife with the cat by her side establishing a mood of tranquility as our eye is led through an open window into a vibrant landscape radiating with high summer sunlight. Bonnard took the Impressionists' experiments with colour to a new pitch and with daring compositional devices was able to give new meaning to a private world of everyday sights and events.

Maine Islands

1922

John Marin

The Phillips family had a very close relationship with John Marin (1870–1953) who was a frequent visitor to Washington as their guest. There are twenty-one of his paintings in the collection. Phillips waxed lyrical about the work of his friend: 'with his amazing intuition he hints at strange truths freshly apprehended' and after his death he wrote 'For half a century of research and urgency he experimented on the frontiers of visual consciousness and his ardours amounted to a joyous dynamic pantheism.' From 1914 Marin regularly went to paint on the coast of Maine where he produced a series of beautiful watercolours. In this work he uses the device of painting a kind of window frame through which we observe the view. It was a technique he initiated in the early 1920s, which provides the work with an added spatial dimension.

Girl with a Plant

1956

Richard
Diebenkorn

During the mid 1950s, just as his Abstract Expressionist works were gaining recognition, Diebenkorn (b. 1922) started painting works with a figurative content. As he himself wrote at this time 'I came to mistrust my desire to explode the picture and supercharge it in some way.' Many of his admirers felt that this return to a degree of representation was a regressive step. However, Diebenkorn did go back to abstraction the following decade. The sparkling Pacific light floods into this painting defining space in blocks, painted with free brushstrokes but within the context of a rigid linear framework. The colour contrast is rich and beautifully harmonized. Within this pictorial context is the girl, isolated and alone. In her hand she holds a flower, a flowing, organic, serpentine shape contrasting with the angularity of the rest of the composition.

Interior with an Egyptian Curtain

1948

Henri Matisse

Matisse (1869–1954) is probably the greatest colourist in twentieth-century painting. From the Fauve experiments of the early years of this century to his cut-out compositions executed when he was too infirm to paint, his work overflows with vibrant colour and dynamic form. This is the last of a series of seven interiors and one of his final easel paintings. Even at the age of seventy-nine, Matisse was still able to paint with an unfailing understanding of colour and pattern.

Here the window is used as a framing element against which is an explosive palm tree. To the right is the powerfully patterned Egyptian curtain, and in front a bowl of pomegranates with a harshly outlined black shadow. What space there is comes out of the interplay of patterns with the formal elements of curtain edge, table and window frame. Freedom of expression and assured control are everywhere in this work. Around the time it was painted Matisse wrote of his method, 'I am simply conscious of the forces I am using and I am driven on by an idea that I can really only grasp as it grows within the picture.' When Matisse visited the Phillips Collection in 1930 he commented that there were five Bonnards hanging in the gallery and only two paintings of his own. When Duncan Phillips said he was planning to add to his collection of the master's works, Matisse remarked that the Phillips were right to have more of Bonnard's work than his own, adding that 'he is the best of us all.'

This adjunct to the National Museum of American Art is devoted to exhibiting works on the decorative arts and crafts. It has a permanent collection of the finest American crafts, including jewellery, glass, ceramics, textiles, woodwork and metalwork. This is exhibited on a rotation basis and there are always temporary exhibitions on similar themes on display. The museum was opened in 1972 and as well as exhibiting the finest in contemporary craft, supports a variety of educational programmes and research fellowships. The Renwick Gallery is continually commissioning new pieces from the best American craftsmen and craftswomen.

The collection is housed in the ornate building in the Second Empire style which was once the home of the Corcoran Gallery and School of Art. Above the main entrance is a cartouche depicting Corcoran and the inscribed motto 'Dedicated to Art'. There are sculptures representing Rubens and Murillo in niches on the facade. It is named after its architect James Renwick who was also responsible for the Castle on the Mall, the headquarters of the Smithsonian Institution and St. Patrick's Cathedral in New York City. Some of the interiors are well worthy of comment, in particular the Grand Salon, probably the finest belle epoque interior in Washington and the Octagon room, an elegant Victorian drawing room decorated with a five-foot-high porcelain vase made in Berlin in the mid nineteenth century. Both rooms are furnished with fine pieces from the 1860s and 1870s, and are hung with a number of portraits and genre paintings by nineteenth-century American artists.

Address
Pennsylvania Avenue and 17th St NW, Washington D.C.
℡ (202) 357 2700

Map reference
㉖

How to get there
Metro: Farragut West

Opening times
Daily 10–5.30. Closed Christmas Day

Entrance fee
Free entrance

Tours
Guided tours available daily 10–1. Tue to Thur 10, 11, 1. Can also be booked at other times, but must be booked in advance. Three weeks notice required

Arthur M. Sackler Gallery of Asian and Near Eastern Art

Address
1050, Independence Ave.
SW, Washington D.C.
© (202) 357 2700.

Map reference
㉗

How to get there
Metro: Smithsonian. Mall or
Independence Avenue exits.

Opening times
Daily 10 to 5.30. Closed
Christmas

Entrance fee
Free entrance

Tours
Daily tours. Enquire at
information desk or call in
advance for daily schedule

With the National Museum of African Art (page 92), the Sackler Gallery makes up the Smithsonian Quadrangle, an underground exhibition space on three levels connected with the Freer Gallery (page 31) by a subterranean exhibition concourse. The aim of the museum is to celebrate the artistic traditions of all the peoples of Asia. Arthur M. Sackler, a medical researcher and philanthropist, became interested in Asian art in the 1950s and thereafter began assiduously collecting first Chinese works of art and then items from other Asian cultures. As a scientist Sackler had his own philosophy regarding collecting: 'Art and science are two sides of the same coin. Science is a discipline pursued with passion; art is a passion pursued with discipline. At pursuing both I have had a lot of fun'. In 1982 he gave one thousand works of Asian art to the Smithsonian and this formed the basis of the museum which opened in 1987.

Two of the great strengths of the collection are the Chinese bronzes and jade objects which formed the basis of Sackler's original gift. In terms of Chinese art there are also extensive collections of lacquerwork and painting. Notable from south and south-east Asia is the temple sculpture and a fine collection of book paintings. Ancient Near Eastern art is also well represented. The dovetailing with the Freer Gallery means that one rarely visits one museum without the other, and there is much which overlaps, not least the education and temporary exhibition programmes. The Sackler Gallery's holdings are much greater than the exhibition space available and so some rotation of exhibitions takes place.

Both the Sackler and Freer Galleries have remarkable collections of Sassanian art, and this piece is one of the finest examples. A rhyton is a horn-shaped drinking vessel, often embellished with the forms of animals as well as human figures. Here a remarkably lifelike image of a young antelope is accompanied by a relief sequence of lion, bull and antelope around the rim of the horn. The astrological symbolism of the animals has been noted and it has been argued that the tree may symbolize fertility.

The Sassanian dynasty was founded in AD 224 by King Ardeshir and its empire eventually controlled not only Persia, but Afghanistan, Syria, Yemen and Egypt. The Empire was, however, destined to be eroded by the rise of Arab power. By the seventh century AD the surge of Islam had swept through Iran and the Sassanian Empire collapsed. In the arts however its influence was profound, setting standards of quality and systems of iconography which guided the development of Iranian art for the next thousand years. Sassanian art gathered up and redefined art forms derived from earlier traditions, not only from ancient Persia but also Assyria, Mesopotamia, Rome and the Hellenistic world. In this respect it forms the bridge between these older traditions and the art of the Islamic world which superseded it.

The Regent Duke Oboi

c.1660

Anonymous Chinese painting

This magnificent silk painting is an Imperial portrait on a grand scale, painted when the subject was at the height of his political career. His blue robes embroidered with golden four-clawed dragons and a two tier golden hat finial with pearls and ruby tip, display Oboi's ducal rank. He belonged to an important Manchu family who rose to high political office during the reign of the Shunzi Emperor (1643–61). Under his reign he was elevated to Duke of the second class. When the Emperor died he was succeeded by his seven-year-old son the Kangxi Emperor, and Oboi attempting to maintain control was elevated to Duke of the first class and granted other honours. However, in June 1669 Oboi was denounced for his excesses and charged with thirty serious crimes. He died in prison, stripped of all his titles and ranks.

The details in this work are very sensitively handled. The weave of the carpet, the peacock feather in the hat and the lacquered chair are fine details. Above all the dignified, rather stern expression on Oboi's face shows this was probably painted from life. Despite its overpowering formality, this painting dates from an interesting period in Chinese art when society was becoming more complex and artistic tastes more heterogeneous. The museum has large holdings of Chinese paintings of high quality from all periods, illustrating a wide range of subject matter.

Some of the least known and most rewarding of Washington's artistic attractions are the grand reception rooms located on the eighth floor of the gaunt 1960s State Department building. The reception rooms are tastefully, and in some cases lavishly, decorated. Originally these rooms were rather dull, but shortly after they began to be used it was decided that a more convivial environment was required for the reception of foreign dignitaries. Under the guidance of Clement E. Conger works of art including exceptionally fine furniture and paintings were collected and the rooms remodelled to resemble the interior of a Palladian country house with suitable mouldings and Venetian windows. All the furniture comes from the period 1725 to 1825 and is American with a few European objects. Notable pieces are the writing desk upon which Thomas Jefferson composed the Declaration of Independence, and an English Sheraton tambour upon which John Jay signed the Treaty of Paris concluding the Revolutionary War. Paintings by John Singleton Copley, Gilbert Stuart, J.B. Greuze and others decorate the walls.

Address
Department of State 23rd and C St NW, Washington D.C.
© (202) 647 3241

Map reference

How to get there
Metro: Foggy Bottom

Opening times
Mon to Fri. Tour hours 9.30, 10.30, 2.45. Closed weekends and holidays

Entrance fee
Free entrance. Children over 12 only

Tours
Guided tours compulsory. Reservations required

TEXTILE MUSEUM

This outstanding specialist museum was founded in 1925 by yet another distinguished private collector, George Hewitt Myers, who was the half-brother of the co-founder of the Bristol Myers pharmaceutical firm. He inherited half of his brother's interest in that company while still a student at Yale University. It was whilst he was an undergraduate there that he bought his first textile, thus commencing a lifelong enthusiasm. The museum was endowed with a quarter of Mr. Myers's considerable fortune on his death.

The museum is a centre for research and scholarship as well as a textile conservation centre. As regards exhibits, which are constantly rotated, the collection is particularly strong on Oriental carpets, Islamic and Coptic textiles, and archaeological textiles from pre-Colombian Peru. There are also extensive collections of Indian, Indonesian, African and Chinese fabrics and works by twentieth-century textile artists from North, Central and South America. The Museum commissions and encourages textile artists active today and experimenting in the medium. As well as collecting and commissioning new work the institution is very concerned with the exhibition of textiles, and displays its exhibits in a remarkably dramatic and informative way.

The collection and research facility is located in two attractive houses near Dupont Circle in central Washington, which was the home of Mr. Myers until his death in 1957. One house was the work of John Russell Pope who designed the National Gallery of Art (page 55), whilst the other, built in 1908, was designed by architect Waddy B. Wood, who also built the adjacent Woodrow Wilson House.

Address
2320 S St NW, Washington D.C.
© (202) 667 0441

Map reference

How to get there
Metro: Dupont Circle

Opening times
Mon to Sat 10–5. Sun 1–5.
Closed: Federal Holidays and December 24

Entrance fee
Suggested contribution $5

This is another distinguished residence associated with George Washington, for it was with his legacy of $8,000 that his step-granddaughter Martha Custis Peter purchased the eight-acre property. Dr William Thornton, the architect of the Capitol and the Octagon House, was instructed to build a house befitting the status of the residents. Many of the furnishings originally came from Mount Vernon and were purchased when the contents were auctioned off in early nineteenth century. Tudor Place is in Georgetown like Dumbarton House (page 26) and Dumbarton Oaks (page 27). Among the other fine buildings in this the oldest part of Washington is the Old Stonehouse, constructed around 1765 – a simple, grey limestone structure containing a small museum. It is located on M street, the main thoroughfare of Georgetown. Don't miss numbers 3001 and 3003, two handsome late eighteenth-century houses. N street boasts a number of the finest Federal period houses in Georgetown; Laird Dunlop House at no 3014 is particularly noteworthy.

Address
1644, 31st Street and R Street, Washington D.C.
✆ Tel: (202) 965 0400

Map reference

How to get there
Metro: Dupont Circle, Foggy Bottom Bus: D2, D4, D6, D8

Opening times
Tue to Sat at guided tour times. Closed Sun, Mon and public holidays

Entrance fee
Suggested donation $5. Students and children $2.50

Tours
Compulsory guided tours Tue to Fri 10, 11.30, 1 and 2.30. Sat tours 10–3

WASHINGTON MONUMENT

Built 1848–88

Address
Centre of the Mall,
Constitution Avenue and
15th St NW, Washington D.C.
✆ (202) 426 6839

Map reference
㉛

How to get there
Metro: Smithsonian

Opening times
From the first Sunday in
April to Labor Day, daily
8am to midnight. Rest of
the year daily 9–5

Entrance fee
Free entrance

Tours
Walk down guided tours Sat
and Sun at 10 and 2

In L'Enfant's original plan for a layout of the city he proposed an equestrian statue of George Washington to be placed at the crossing of the north-south axis, linking the Mall with the White House and the east-west axis of the Capitol. However, it was not until 1832 that the Washington National Monument Society was formed. They raised money and held a competition for a suitable design, which was won by Robert Mills. The foundation stone was laid in 1848. Work ceased from the outbreak of the Civil War to resumption of construction in 1876 and although the same stone from a Maryland quarry was used in its construction, one can still see the point at which work was started again as it has a subtly different colour. The Monument was eventually opened to the public in 1888. At that time it was the tallest building in the world, soon to be overtaken by the Eiffel Tower. The Obelisk still dominates the city skyline and is the tallest structure in central Washington.

L'Enfant originally conceived his 'President's House' on the lines of a grand palace, but the design eventually chosen was that of James Hoban, an Irish architect who proposed the more modest Palladian mansion. In 1814 the House was burned by the British and Hoban was forced to demolish the old White House and rebuild from scratch. The House has been altered and renovated many times since its construction, but still retains its original form. The interior decorations have changed frequently in accordance with the tastes of the respective Presidents and their families. Since Jaqueline Kennedy was first lady 1961–63, there has been a concerted effort to acquire items of historic and artistic interest. The public has access to a number of the rooms on the ground and first floors. As one would expect there is an excellent collection of presidential portraits together with other paintings of the eighteenth and nineteenth centuries. Furnishings are also worth noting, particularly the examples of French Empire style furniture in the Red Room and the English furniture in the State Dining Room.

Address

1600, Pennsylvania Avenue NW, Washington D.C.
✆ (202) 456 1414/ (202) 456 7041

Map reference

How to get there

Metro: Farragut West, McPherson Square

Opening times

Tue to Sat 10–12. Closed Thanksgiving, Christmas, New Years Day, during state visits.

Entrance fee

Free, but tickets (available from booths on the Ellipse) are required Mar to Sept

WOODLAWN

Built 1799–1805

Address
9000 Richmond Highway, Alexandria, Virginia
✆ (703) 780 4000

Map reference
㉝

How to get there
Metro to Huntingdon Station. Transfer to the 9A Bus to Fort Belvoir which stops at Woodlawn.

Opening times
9.30 to 4.30. Closed New Years Day, Thanksgiving, Christmas Day.

Entrance fee
Adults $6, children and seniors $4. Combination ticket with Pope Leighey House $10 and $6.50.

Woodlawn holds an important place in the hearts of those interested in the early days of the American republic. The land once belonged to George Washington but was ceded to his nephew and Eleanor Parae Custis, a granddaughter whom George and Martha had raised since early childhood. After their marriage they built Woodlawn, which still contains many of the original furnishings which belonged to the family as well as others from the epoch which were added at a later date. The grounds are also impressive with parterres and a large park stretching down to the River Potomac.

In the grounds of Woodlawn is a delightful small wooden house built by Frank Lloyd Wright in 1941. One of his so called Usonian houses, it was conceived as an inexpensive house that ordinary people could afford, using simple materials such as wood and brick. All the furniture in the house was designed by Wright and there are some delightful decorative details which are unmistakeably his. The house, with its strong horizontals and spatial unity, bears all the hallmarks of Wright's design.

The author and publisher would like to thank the following Washington museums and galleries, individuals and photographic archives for their kind permission to use the following illustrations:

Hirshhorn Museum and Sculpture Garden, Smithsonian Institution, Gift of Joseph H.Hirshhorn, 1966 (Photos. Lee Stalsworth): 6 (© ARS, New York and DACS. London 1995), 40a (© Mrs B.Lipkin, London), 40b, 41, 42a & b, 43 (© ADAGP, Paris and DACS, London 1995), 44 (© ADAGP, Paris and DACS, London 1995), 45a (© DACS 1995), 45b (© ADAGP, Paris and DACS, London 1995), 46 (© The Henry Moore Foundation)

National Gallery of Art, © 1994 Board of Trustees: 7l (Ailsa Mellon Bruce Fund), 7r (Widener Collection), 8l (Samuel H.Kress Collection), 9a (Andrew W.Mellon Collection), 9b (John Hay Whitney Collection), 12 (Chester Dale Collection), 13a (Andrew W.Mellon Collection), 15b (© Estate of David Smith/DACS, London/VAGA, New York 1995), 57 (Samuel H.Kress Collection), 58 (Samuel H.Kress Collection), 59 (Widener Collection), 60 (Andrew W.Mellon Collection), 61 (Ailsa Mellon Bruce Fund), 62 (Andrew W.Mellon Collection), 63 (Andrew W.Mellon Collection), 64 (Widener Collection), 65 (Samuel H.Kress Collection), 66 (Andrew W.Mellon Collection), 67 (Samuel H.Kress Collection), 68 (Andrew W.Mellon Collection), 69 (Widener Collection), 70 (Andrew W.Mellon Collection), 71a (Andrew W.Mellon Collection), 71b (Samuel H.Kress Collection), 72a & b (Samuel H.Kress Collection), 73 (Ailsa Mellon Bruce Fund), 74 (Widener Collection), 75 (Andrew W.Mellon Collection), 76 (Samuel H.Kress Collection), 77 (Andrew W.Mellon Collection), 78 (Gift of Mrs Mellon Bruce in memory of her father, Andrew W.Mellon), 79 (Samuel H.Kress Collection), 80 (Samuel H.Kress Collection), 81 (Andrew W.Mellon Collection), 82 (Ferdinand Lammot Belin Fund), 83 (Harris Whittemore Collection), 84a (Gift of Mr and Mrs Cornelius Vanderbilt Whitney), 84b (Gift of the Avalon Foundation), 85 (Gift of Horace Havemeyer in memory of his mother, Louisine W.Havemeyer), 86 (Chester Dale Collection), 87 (Chester Dale Collection), 88 (Chester Dale Collection), 89 (Chester Dale Collection © DACS 1995), 90 (Ailsa Mellon Bruce Fund © ARS, New York and DACS, London 1995), 91 (Gift of

Mr and Mrs William Howard Adams © 1995 The Andy Warhol Foundation for the Visual Arts, Inc.)

National Portrait Gallery, Smithsonian Institution: 8r (owned jointly with Museum of Fine Arts, Boston), 13b (Gift of Paul Mellon), 102 (owned jointly with Museum of Fine Arts, Boston), 103a, 103b (reprinted with permission of Joanna T.Steichen), 104

Angelo Hornak, London: 10

Courtesy of the Freer Gallery of Art, Smithsonian Institution: 11 (04.75), 32 (04.61), 33a (17.182), 33bl&r (49.20/49.21), 34 (29.84), 35 (45.9)

The Phillips Collection: 14, 107, 108, 109, 110, 111, 112a, 112b (© ADAGP/SPA-DEM, Paris and DACS, London 1995), 113a, 113b, 113c, 114(© Succession H.Matisse/DACS, London 1995)

Courtesy of the Arthur M.Sackler Gallery, Smithsonian Institution: 15a (S1986.400), 117 (S1987.33), 118 (S1991.93)

Nicholas Reese: 16, 18, 19, 20, 21, 26, 27, 31, 36, 37, 39, 47, 48, 50, 51, 52, 53, 54, 55, 56, 92, 94, 97, 101, 105, 106, 115, 116, 119, 120, 121, 122, 123, 124

The Corcoran Museum of Art: 22 (William A.Clark Collection), 23 (William A.Clark Collection), 23a (Gift of William Wilson Corcoran), 24b (Museum Purchase, Gallery Fund), 25 (Museum Purchase)

Dumbarton Oaks Research Library and Collections: 28, 29, 30

Hillwood Museum: 38

The Kreeger Museum (photo. Franko Khoury): 49

National Museum of African Art, Eliot Elisofon Archives, Smithsonian Institution (photo.Bruce Fleischer): 93

National Museum of American Art (Art Resource, New York): 95, 96

The National Museum of Women in the Arts: 98, 99a, 99b (© ADAGP, Paris and DACS, London 1995), 100a (© DACS 1995), 100b (© ARS, New York and DACS, London 1995)

The author would like to thank Caroline Bugler and Julia Brown at Studio Editions for their help and advice, Clive and Helen Harris for looking after me in Washington, Eric Shanes for his ideas and enthusiasm, Lucy Davies and Natasha Bult for their assistance with the photographs, and Nick Bell and Tracy Forster for their patient tolerance whilst I was writing.

INDEX

Index of Artists, Sculptors and Architects
Figures in bold refer to main entries

INDEX

A note on the itineraries

The following itineraries are designed for those with a week in Washington, and for practical reasons museums or buildings that are near each other have been grouped together on the same day. Although it should be possible to view all the items suggested on each day's itinerary, visitors may well choose to proceed at a more leisurely pace and concentrate on one or two of the suggested items while excluding others. Those with limited time should focus on starred items. Works of art are listed in the order that they are most likely to be seen within each museum or gallery. The numbers in circles beside each location are map references.

As regards public transport, all appropriate metro stops have been indicated where they are in close proximity to the gallery or museum. Where buses provide alternatives they have been mentioned. Washington, however, like many American cities is car orientated and there is ample parking in the central area where most of the sites of artistic interest are located. The metro is the most convenient mode of transport to use in the centre but museums located in the suburbs such as Hillwood and the Kreeger Museum are really only easily accessible by car or taxi. Similarly, Alexandria and the Mount Vernon area are best visited by car. At all the outlying galleries and country houses there are ample parking facilities. In the centre of Washington there are three hour limit free parking spaces, as well as parking meters and downtown car parks at reasonable rates. Opening times and entry prices are correct at the time of publication, but may be liable to change without notice.

DAY 1 MORNING

✪ THE NATIONAL GALLERY OF ART ⑱ (p.55)

West Building (p.55)
The Calling of the Apostles Andrew and Peter
Duccio di Buoninsegna (p.57)
The Adoration of the Magi
Fra Angelico/ Fra Filippo Lippi (p.58)
The Youthful David
Andrea del Castagno (p.59)
The Adoration of the Magi
Sandro Botticelli (p.60)
✪ **Ginevra di Benci**
Leonardo da Vinci (p.61)
The Crucifixion
Pietro Perugino (p.62)
✪ **The Alba Madonna**
Raphael (p.63)
The Feast of the Gods
Giovanni Bellini and Titian (p.64)
The Adoration of the Shepherds
Giorgione (p.65)
Venus with a Mirror
Titian (p.66)
Apollo Pursuing Daphne
Giovanni Battista Tiepolo (p.67)
The Needlewoman
Diego Velázquez (p.68)

A Young Girl with her Duenna
Bartolomé Esteban Murillo (p.69)
The Annunciation
Jan van Eyck (p.70)
Portrait of a Lady
Rogier van der Weyden (p.71)
The Temptation of Saint Anthony
Peter Bruegel the Elder (p.71)
Christ on the Cross
Mathis Grünewald (p.72)
Portrait of a Clergyman
Albrecht Dürer (p.72)
Daniel in the Lions Den
Sir Peter Paul Rubens (p.73)
Descent from the Cross
Rembrandt van Rijn (p.74)
Girl with the Red Hat
Jan Vermeer (p.75)
Italian Comedians
Antoine Watteau (p.76)
The House of Cards
Jean-Baptiste-Siméon Chardin (p.77)
Young Girl Reading
Jean-Honoré Fragonard (p.78)
Napoleon
Jacques-Louis David (p.79)
Madame Moitessier
Jean-Auguste-Dominique Ingres (p.80)
Mortlake Terrace
Joseph Mallord William Turner (p.81)